Thou Shalt Not Covet

Thou Shalt Not Covet

Megan Kaufmunn, Ph.D.

VANTAGE PRESS
New York

FIRST EDITION

All rights reserved, including the right of
reproduction in whole or in part in any form.

Copyright © 1997 by Megan Kaufmunn, Ph.D.

Published by Vantage Press, Inc.
516 West 34th Street, New York, New York 10001

Manufactured in the United States of America
ISBN: 0-533-11909-X

Library of Congress Catalog Card No.: 96-90111

0 9 8 7 6 5 4 3 2 1

Dedicated
to
David Bernard Jarrett, M.D.
Athens, Georgia

Through all the pain and sorrow I have endured, and yet to encounter, I will never find a better friend than I have found in you. Thousands upon thousands of hours will transcend but you will always be remembered, for it was you who created the light's path to shine so brightly down within my tunnel of darkness. Your patience, your dedication, your ethics, your perseverance, your determination to believe in me, to recognize the times when I had no strength, no desire to continue my struggle, are attributes found in few.

Thank you, thank you . . . The words are too simple for what you have enabled me to become, and yet I can find no words that would equate with the gift given to me—a gift so rare, so unique that it is almost as if I turned around one day to unexpectedly find your guidance as I sifted through the grains of sand composing my life, and never once did you turn away. Thank you for being there the many times I ran away from my inner pain. Never was there a time when I was once again ready to scoop and sift that I did not find you there awaiting my return.

You are truly my knight in shining armor; and if a wish cast upon the brightest star could manifest itself, I would wish to pass onto another this gift of living which you have so graciously presented to me. Your gift is one I will cherish forever. Thank you for the greatest gift one could share.

With all my heart,
Megan
September 18, 1995

Thou Shalt Not Covet

Prologue

There needed to be an eleventh commandment: "Thou shalt not covet thy child, abuse thy child, terrorize thy child, rape thy child." Often I have wondered why these were not addressed; and had they been, would there have been many, many less children upon the face of this earth? And then, when the evil surpassed the good, there would be no laughter, no joy to fill the air between the clouds and the soil.

There are children across the world who no longer laugh, no longer dream, no longer trust. They have been victimized by others—often, their own parents. When that occurs, the child must find a method of survival. For me, it was the splitting of my personality into other me's who could absorb the pain and the terror—me's who could nurture my wounds, internally and externally; who could experience the emotions involved when the core chose to shut down; and who could keep some sense of the past neatly shelved within the mind until its processing came due. The me's could be called upon without notice, without refusal, without accountability, a beckoning to be answered without exception and always returned to the core at closure.

These different me's have forever been there amidst the cracks and crevices, folded as influential particles of my memory. Always, always present—sometimes passively, sometimes aggressively, but always present, lingering in wait for just that precise moment when one of the many clones would emerge to take control of a life so toiled and disoriented. Many times the clones appeared to be someone else, but were mirror images of me—the same eyes, the same hair, the same nose—everything reflective except the emotions. They were little me's of different ages during those times when life was most difficult, the times I wished so hard to be blotted from my memory. It was those clones who disturbed me immensely as I ran from refuge to refuge, always seated safely away from reach while he prodded and ripped at a little girl's body until he finished, laughed, and walked away. But things were different in my refuge, for there was no pain and no one could reach us.

There will be a time when all the me's will be fully integrated into the core as a whole person. There will be more smiles, more laughs with meaning, more hope for the future. This terror, this abuse had taken decades from life, and it would be a slow, painful walk along this path until the integration of the me's would be complete.

Sexual abuse is one of those things from which children don't "bounce back" without pain and scarring. It's that moment of stolen innocence in which a child suddenly learns what the adult world is about, yet lacks the cognitive skills to understand. It's one of those times when a parent severely scars a child physically and psychologically, evoking lasting emotional traps that surface and resurface time after time, never appearing to end with their eternal torture.

The trauma, and the repetition of that trauma, is graphically described as remembered and experienced year by year. The following pages are not intended for young readers, but rather for the thousands of adults who are, or who have been, abused by the dysfunctional adults in their lives. The trauma still returns from time to time. Holidays and special occasions are always difficult and, at times, fearful—not fearful of a reccurrence, but rather that once again my mind will begin to search for "why." It is that endless pondering for unanswered whys that compels me from one day to another, knowing the answer will never be found; and, the risk of my becoming suicidal remains ever-present. The events unfold in horror... horror so traverse at moments that grasping reality as it should be, rather than as it was, developed a tunnel of hope in which survival was manageable. Survival from one terror to the next was the motivating force keeping me alive during years of abuse. The memories are not pleasant and the extent of the abuse and torture maximize from beginning to end. My acceptance of these memories is with much difficulty and pain.

Therapy and the writing of this book have released much of the harbored resentment stored deep within my memory and soul. It is the hope of this writer to instill in all adults an intense desire to keep every child safe.

CHAPTER 1

The relentless flood of memories stormed my thoughts, terrorizing me with the harsh reality lying dormant in my soul. Sleepless nights and depressed days became parasitic upon my ruined and destined life.

Nearly three decades have passed since that cold Christmas Eve buried deep with me, that dark destructive secret when the innocence of childhood was stolen away. Traumatized and alone, I waited the eternal hours of the night, watching as dawn broke gently amidst the snow-laden treetops, reflecting subtly the fresh, unblemished arrival of morning. Tainted and courageless, I searched for understanding.

Quite early that Christmas, I found the shower to be my haven. Sobbing and scrubbing beneath the steaming waters, I found no cleansing effect. The tears, the scrubbing, the pounding streams of water—nothing reversed time. Confusion, violation, betrayal! Each compelled my desperate search for logic as his smell, his touch, his words were permanently ingrained in my visual image, flashing over and over, refusing to relinquish their magnetic hold. The horror, forever bound within my senses, stalked my being as thieves' steps upon the darkened night. How could this memory subside when all else in life felt so meaningless, so cold? Suddenly, the change in the hot, steamy water to the cold, icy hatred of the night jolted within me life's reality. Panic consumed my mind as I feared his return.

Slowly, fearfully, I gently nurtured my bruised, battered self, crying silently for another life—somewhere else. I wanted to sleep, to dream, to forget. Climbing into bed, the odor of the linens provoked vivid flashbacks. In a silent haste of hate, I ripped the linens from the bed, hoping to discard his lustful play. Sleep! My mind cried out for the seclusion of reality. Sleep would prohibit his intrusion. Only distorted thoughts prohibited my sleep. The quietness of the house sparked hope. This was only an uncontrolled moment never to be repeated. This was my father, my hero. Why had he done this? How had I made him so angry? Amidst my questions, I only found confusion. I would be okay if only my mind would sleep. Please, please—just let my mind sleep.

 I sensed movement within the room. Suddenly, in the pit of my stomach came that gnawing, churning twist, sinking my heart to the pits of hell. I stared at the approaching figure. There was a strangeness about his unfamiliar glances as he silently thrust his desires upon me. My mind screamed! His robe dropped onto the floor. Without notice, I was floating toward a shelf up above, which seemed to have always been there awaiting my occupancy—an invisible shelf just out of reach, safe within the layers of air, resting until its use was no longer needed by the victim of his onslaught. Whether it would start from the right or left, the invisible shelf would quickly appear, remaining for as long as necessary—minutes, hours, days, weeks. . . . Always it stayed until life was manageable once more. It was a familiar shelf of comfort, far removed from him. A friend for life, adding confusion as I looked down upon the transgressions, recording each and every detail deep within my memory, surviving to experience the pain and desolation endured by that other me, shocked and whimpering far below. But there was no one else there to hear the soft whimpers of that little tormented soul.

His mouth touched hers as he ripped clothing from a shaking, mortified, and defenseless body. Inwardly, she cried as his mouth went to her breasts—biting, sucking, pulling. Paralyzed, she gave no response to his lustful moves. Quickly, he buried his face between her legs, thrusting his tongue in, out, and along her genitals. Working his mouth up to her breasts, he forcibly entered her. Tears flowed hurriedly across her face as his penis thrust in and out, in and out. Repeatedly, he moaned loudly, demanding, "What am I doing? What am I doing?"

The mournful creature shouted, "You're hurting me!" Expecting him to halt, she prepared for the pain to end. Angrily, he grabbed her face with his hands, piercing his eyes down into hers as he shoved his penis deep within her, laughingly thrusting back and forth. His hands squeezed her breasts; his mouth whispered nasty sexual statements until he gave one final thrust, collapsing on top of the whimpering child. With the silence brought by his halted actions, it was time for the one upon the shelf to come down to the other me and mend her broken thoughts before putting her safely to bed for sleep.

He lay there by her side for hours, frequently inserting his hand inside as if guarding her close proximity. His mouth resting on still rather underdeveloped breasts was confusing. There was no reason why he should be sexually aroused by this child. How could any man find his own child sexually stimulating? As her mind raced ahead of her, she realized three days remained before anyone would return from holiday visits. Attempting to find an escape ended with his startles. Stirring next to her was the beast she had learned to hate in less than a day. Patiently, she awaited his departure, affording her a safe return to her haven. Once there, her mind would temper the lingering filth, for deep inside there was a yearning to be clean—to wash his lust away.

Christmas is such a beautiful time of the year, with the multicolored lights, carols, bright-colored paper, satin ribbons, and bells ringing softly through the air, accompanying the snowflakes floating quietly to the ground. Its eve, always decorated with excitement, was frosted this year by the cold, cold snowy air. Snuggled under the warm covers and all alone, it seemed like a nightmare—not something that had really happened. But, then, there was that feeling in the back of my mind that said it had. There was a numbness in the silence of the house and I wondered if I would be okay. I wondered if I was the only living person in the whole world. Where was God during this? There was no one except the one just like me—the one upon the shelf.

Standing beneath the hot, steamy waters, I searched for cleanliness, but my attempts to restore my sanity failed. Horror struck as the beast stepped inside the shower. I questioned why he was doing this, but no acknowledgment was granted; or perhaps I missed it as I journeyed through the air to my invisible shelf. Looking down, I watched as he placed his lips on hers, kissing passionately, remarking, "It's Daddy's responsibility to teach his little girl about sex."

His fingers moved across her buttocks. Pulling her onto his body, he moved his penis toward her rectum. Unsuccessful, he became angry. Ordering her onto the floor of the shower, he pushed his penis deep into her mouth, shouting, "Suck!"

Timidly, she moved away hoping to escape. Violently, he shoved her against the shower wall. There was nothing to do but comply. Each time she decreased suction or stopped altogether, he thrust his penis deeper into her throat, as if trying to choke her. Fearfully, she followed his instructions until his passion exploded inside her mouth. The sadness was overwhelming as I looked tenderly down upon her from the shelf high above. It would soon be time to take the other me into my arms, tenderly mend her broken thoughts once again, and put her to sleep within my mind.

I don't remember how long I sat beneath the streams of water too stunned to move. The water was icy cold, but then, my whole life felt cold and lonely. Within my body, were vile remnants fighting to destroy its shell of evilness, as the total silence of the house beckoned me out. Exhausted, I fell asleep. I wanted to sleep, to forget. But within minutes, his image shattered my escape. The ivory-colored object in his hand was of unknown nature to my mind. Quickly, I searched for the shelf.

His passionate kissing of her breasts, mouth, and neck erupted once again. Quietly, he whispered instructions for her to roll over onto her stomach. His kissing continued across her back and buttocks. His quivering tongue moved across her rectum, building a saliva residue. He spread her buttocks, as if trying to extend his tongue as deeply inside her as possible. It seemed like hours when he grasped the object, pushing it into her rectum. She protested violently, struggling to free the intrusive object, only to find her refusal to comply leaving her tied in restraints, blocking any further attempts to disobey. Her demands to know why merited a repugnant, "I want my dick up your ass when I'm ready for it!" She didn't know a lot about sex, but she did know this was painful and frightening. Fearful of dying, she followed his every command as the other me waited for her chance to return.

Several years I had searched for a meaning to life and found none. Now it seemed completely impossible to live. The thought had passed through my head many times before, but now it was different. It wasn't passing. It was lingering, absorbing the silent powers of the contentment it would bring—the end to pain, the end to terror, the end to him. He had made me frightening to myself, taking whatever he wished from me. Destruction—bit by bit—was his goal. That's what my life had been, and now he had succeeded. Surely death would commence soon.

Hours passed. The dreams erupted, sending me back to that wonderful shelf of comfort. Upon his return, there was a razor in his hand. He placed his nude body over her chest, laying his penis on her mouth. "Suck my dick, little girl. Suck Daddy's dick and make it hard."

She followed his instructions. He watched closely her facial expression as his penis grew inside her mouth. Smiling, he withdrew his penis. Kissing and drooling around her breasts, he pulled each nipple with his teeth, working his way down to her pubic hair. Inserting his tongue into her vagina, he fondled her, raising himself only to see her expression.

Picking up the razor, he began to shave her genitals. Frightened of her violator, she lay in paralyzed silence. Each time the smooth skin was revealed, he became more and more aroused. With all pubic hair removed and him at a full erection, he pulled the object from her rectum. Pushing his thighs under her buttocks, his penis entered her rectum. Momentarily, she felt the warmth of his ejaculation mixing with her blood. She was learning young the smells of sex, particularly that of blood. Instantaneously, his mouth and tongue went to her smooth genitals. Minutes later he left her tied, abused, and massively confused. Perhaps the only reason for his departure was pure physical exhaustion. Defenseless, she recited Hail Mary after Hail Mary.

Hours later the cords restricting my defense were cut. Again, I found my haven in the shower. Sobbing, scrubbing, and clawing my body raw did nothing to lessen the dirtiness. My battered mind had but one thought—survive the moment. Somehow, I thought there would be someone to help me, someone to keep me safe from the person whom I had always wanted to be my hero.

Sadly, and without control, she relived the violations upon an unwilling soul—the force he used, the pain she endured. Tears flowed across her cheeks like spring rivers flowing from snow-infested mountains, hurrying to find a finality to their force. But all the soap and water in the world could not remove the filthy coating of her body, so tainted with the acts of his passion.

Looking down on her, it was easy to see the bloodiness of a crime too taboo for discussion. Blood was everywhere about her genitals and thighs, leaving large splotches of its brightness against the linens. There was a lot of blood—perhaps, too much. Its sight brought about great queasiness. Blood stays inside the body, that she knew. She also knew there was too much blood being revealed. That's why death would commence shortly. All she needed to do was wait. She looked so dreadfully scared and hurt as he pounded away at her, screaming obscenities throughout his brutal attacks. This, too, would subside.

The next two days were uneventful. I had to believe this would never happen again. My mind was terrorizing my soul! How I wished none of this had taken place. I had to convince myself—to believe none of this was real.

As soon as my mother returned from her holiday visit, I described for her what my father had done, pleading with her to halt his actions. Never making eye contact with me, she calmly said, "That's one of those things you learn to live with."

Her comment was the most devastating acknowledgment of my abuse. The person who should have protected me chose to look the other way. I vowed never to cry again as long as my lungs breathed the stenchful air. The sensitivity of my age would make me recant that vow as my father's demands and my hopes bounced up and down on my carousel of life, leaving splitting after splitting from my core. And with the igniting of each splitting, I wished my soul's release, quietening this forbidden nightmare.

CHAPTER 2

Haunting memories became my constant companion. Life's rules had changed. I no longer knew how to play. Racing thoughts bombarded my thinking. What had I done? Why did he rape me? Why had things changed? I wanted my life to be different, not as it had become. Why were some things so irreversible?

Walking through the house created dreadful fear as simple sounds provoked trembles and rapid breathing. Living had slowly returned to that atmosphere of horror. Each minute capsuled the potential of another brutal violation. It's that indescribable moment suspended in air awaiting the plunge of the roller coaster that recklessly jerks your stomach at the top only to feel its retrieval as it slams laughingly into your drained body in the depths. Suspense, and fear of the unpredictable tarnished my life. A life filled with unknown and unwanted variables—all controlled by my rapist.

Unpredictability—that was the failing element. The randomness of its surprise. The mother who no longer plays the sexual partner for her spouse. Oh, how that surprise shreds a child's hope for life. Crushing and demoralizing, it is the surprise that sends one to the bottom of the pit, groping in the darkness, unable to find the entrance to the tunnel leading out. A tunnel with no light at the other end.

My father was gone. My mother, present with her paralyzing gaze, summoned all her hate for me. Never a spoken word, but always a chilling look, the kind you give when you despise one's very presence. I do not know why she hated me, why she didn't want me, or why she did nothing to protect me. It was those same paralyzing looks that made me hide from her, the ones that made me sleep under my bed when I was younger.

Plagued by confusion, frustration, and memories, the internal battlefield of my being was staged. Obsessive-compulsive thought patterns held the only entrance to the realistic perception of my world. Sleep became my enemy. It allowed the invasion of his memories—his touch, his smell, his voice, his image. His presence terrorized my soul. Each morning spurred the battle onward; evenings replayed the battle. The reliving of his rapes night after night was taking its toll. It was those moments when the battle appeared to have little significance. It was also those moments when something within me struggled to live. My mind could be my friend. Concentration diminished sleep, which in turn diminished the memories. It appeared to be a workable solution. It was to become a life-long behavior developing greater complexity with the passage of time.

Seven days had passed in which I eluded further abuse, although moments transpired when it appeared my rapist would begin once again. Unsure of what deterred him, I distanced myself. Scared at the thought of more rapes, I needed time to comprise a strategy as my bruised, battered body was healing. My mind was not. Its crevices were becoming more and more stocked with their damage. If only my mind would convince itself that the last week never occurred, if my body would heal faster, if my spirit could be rebuilt, or if someone could pull me from this dark, lonely pit, then it would all be okay.

My silent search within the darkness created passive pleas for help going unnoticed. Time again was stalking my being. That uncontrollable variable playing havoc with a life on the threshold of despair. I knew he would return—a gut feeling I had learned to abhor. Waiting, waiting, waiting. The tugging pain of waiting, second only to the pain of lust. The pain that ended one pain always commenced another. Which was worse? The anguish of the anticipation or the rapes of lust? He was the hunter. I was his prey. I felt every moment of his intense hunt. The increasing pains of horror as someone is following, stalking, manipulating every finished move. That heart-pounding sensation of knowing someone is closely watching every step surrounding you on all sides as panic floods your brain awaiting death. It's like being thrown over the side of a mountain, but you don't hit bottom. You just tumble and tumble, gaining speed each time. You sense the strong impact with the earth, visualizing your blood-splattered body becoming putty against the sullen soil. The thought alone mortifies your soul. It's more effective than the actual impact. It's the anticipation that destroys and manipulates without actual violations.

Mind games. He was playing mind games with a child not yet fully exposed to the world. Experiential background, the interaction which prepares us for the real world. He clearly had the advantage. Therefore, I had to be fast in every reply, every gesture, yet stay within the perimeters that assured the least violations. Perhaps the safest route was that of silence. Voicing internally the pain and frustration would keep me more safe than if I opposed my hunter. The silent hunt had commenced. There would be no winners in this hunt, only shattered lives trying to glue together the few remaining pieces. I waited for dawn.

Shadows danced in the early morning sun, adorning the snow with shaded figures, like the quiet calm in the eye of the storm. The sun tells every movement the wind transgresses. That slow easy swaying from side to side, acknowledging the flexibility of life as well as the blatant line of limitations. That was the crossroads where I stood. A crossroads where understanding was not possible, where the instilling of destructive seeds was probable. I wanted many times to hide in the dark, dark shadows, encasing myself with safety. There appeared to be some kind of love enveloped in these solemn statues of suspense, holding treasures that only time reveals. The passive change as the sun liberates their growth only to suction them across that invisible line of time once again.

There were many invisible lines crossing, like the boundaries between a parent and a child, the boundaries between sex and lust, and the boundaries between rational and irrational behaviors. The boundary not yet crossed was that between life and death. Death had merely left stabbings along the way. Death would patronize life, allowing time and yet being mindful that it lurks closely somewhere in some form for all of us. The difference is in the pace. If you have a slow-moving timepiece, you have more time between the stabbings than if you have a fast one. Whether my rapist was a slow hunter or a fast hunter, I had not yet determined. Time, and only time, would tell.

CHAPTER 3

The mind drifts back in times of trauma, perhaps in search of logic, of hope, of comfort, of familiarity; mine sifted through the clutter of my life day by day, looking for all of those. Often, it seemed insane as it rehashed specific events. All these years I had thought of myself as the different one, especially when the terrifying thoughts surfaced. Only now I know they were not thoughts; they were real and horrible. And they did happen to me.

Tears of relief rolled down my cheeks, for at long last, I knew I wasn't crazy. I did remember; but, sadly, I also realized my mind had not been playing tricks on me. Rather, it had been trying to allow the truth to surface. All those times I thought I was wrong, mistaken, only to learn I was right after all.

Carefully thinking back, I found an error along the way, in that children assume their parents love them; but what happens when that parent does not or cannot? I tried hard to believe I was loved—by someone. It's a belief one wants to have as years pass, for the simple reason of being part of something. It helps one with believing in one's self, if nothing else. Some children have it and others do not. I did not.

Internally, deep inside, I perceived my unwantedness. Life was a search for just one person to want me, one person to love me. Maybe this was how it was supposed to be, and all the bad feelings I experienced were my fault. But my heart yearned for the missing unfamiliar elements that just seemed to be lacking. The void I sensed was unfamiliar, yet haunting. Like a lost spaceship eternally circling in the great universe, failing to leave its orbit. The speed of life was constant, accelerated, with its resultant effect a slow, steady death.

I had become their prisoner, locked away from emotional growth. A prisoner in a system with no accountability. I thought back to the first time I found a need for my invisible shelf, floating upward onto it to rest, to process the pain.

My mind was tired today, it hurt to think. It appeared to be all cluttered from the plundering of life. A whole consortium of events intermixed with varying time elements jerking me and my world from one era to another, leaping through several years and then reverting. The confusion made my head hurt, a familiar hurt from my past. Only time would ease the pain, time and the sorting of each event neatly into its respective file. There were many files to be neatly shelved within my mind. Files of sadness sitting prim and proper on designated shelves of silence.

Perhaps that is where the many me's originated. Always there had been more than one of me hiding within the tissues of my brain. They were silent beings at first, with the controlling power exerting from their eyes. Frightened eyes filled with hate, big eyes always demanding of attention. They were more noticeable during times when my mind was cluttered. Even the world appeared distant to me, as if I wasn't a part of it, but rather, an observer just marking time as everyone else experienced the events. They knew the actual impact of all the feelings—I knew only the observations. Much resigned to accepting events, I watched the different me's develop within my mind. At least this way, they hurt from the pain. All I had to do was watch them hurt until I could let them once again go away.

The many me's distressed my being with disturbed and conflicted messages. Most of them were angry and aggressive with only a few offering hope. Why some offered hope is still much of a puzzle, but I surmised the aggressive ones hated me for having passed the actual pain onto them. The me's became victims sustaining my survival. Victims with whom I communicated by looks and thoughts in a world of silence. The me's became more and more diversified, struggling to maintain an air of sanity with each consecutive depression.

Each time the anger attached itself deep inside my stomach lining, I experienced the weightlessness as I floated safely above his reach to nestle upon the invisible shelf high above his cruel and imposed acts. That was the creation of the many me's, the source of my guilt. Somehow through their creation, never did I feel the actual pain and the overwhelming sadness that filled their eyes, only the observed pain. But it wasn't just he who initiated the abuse. His wife also ignited some of the me's.

Looking down, she saw the toddler rigidly wedged between the wall and toilet, silently awaiting the onslaught of anger. Her tiny thumb thrust between her lips rested snugly upon her tongue as her forefinger hooked around her nose. Tears flowed quietly down her cheeks, puddling in the little clenched fist as her eyes became plastered upon her mother. Her dark black curls dripped with water from her most recent dip into the bowl. It was her thumb that always seemed to get her there. Sucking her thumb was irritating to her mother for some reason never established within the cognitions of this two-year-old. Always she felt more secure with her thumb inside her mouth. It was a way of crying silently when one's mouth was shoved full. It also kept the finger retracted from pointing, or, worse, raising the arms to be lifted hopefully by someone who cared. It also prevented the mouth from uttering words like "Mama" or "blankie."

The thumb functioned as a safety valve. And with this tyrant, it was necessary to always have the valve set.

Often the mind has searched its knowledge for discernment of why the tyrant did not drown the toddler, why she always lifted her out prior to that point. Perhaps this was her punishment for sucking her thumb, or did the tyrant just not have that element for instant murder? Or had this just been an intended slow abuse to total destruction decades later? Her intent was trivial, but the resultant emotional damage was not. The confusion and desolation must have been much like that of the toddler as her head crashed down inside the toilet bowl, forcing water into the mouth and nose.

The red marks on her forehead became bigger and bigger, or maybe they were bruises from the hard blows. The lack of help from the small hands clutching the toilet seat provided no relief from the deadly blows. The water filled her nostrils forcing open her mouth. It was cold water, shocking to its touch. The kind of cold that catches your breath despite anticipation. It would all stop soon, so those tiny hands could wipe away the wetness pressing back the curls falling into her eyes. Hopefully, she would be dry in a while and could cuddle her blankie close to her thumb securely tucked away inside her mouth.

It would be nap time. A time when no one would hurt her for a while. A time she would spend in the room of the attic after she was thrown onto the bare floor and the door slammed mightily behind her. Always when the door to the room was closed so was the pain.

It was nice to have everything closed away. The calmness of the room left time for her mind to forget the acts of the day. It was much more comfortable when the curls were dry and the tears all gone. The only moisture was that around the thumb, the connecting element for security. Perhaps it was security that this toddler craved deep within her shallow being. But no one knew, for the answer was locked inside of this tiny creature whose only recognizable goal was survival. She is the smallest of the me's, always wedged in that corner except when closed within the bare room for her naps. The closed windows obstructed the sun from sharing its lovely warmth of life upon the cold unfriendly air. The toddler must have yearned to feel the closeness of the sun, to feel its rays reaching down, much like the tentacles of the octopus flowing gracefully through the ocean waters. Somehow those waters seemed accepting, warm, needed by the toddler. It appeared she wanted to be a part of that world rather than hers. There was hope in that world, someone to help her. There was no one to help her now. She was, indeed, in a world all by herself, struggling with unsurmountable odds. Someday, somehow, someone would save her—maybe.

I knew then there were more parts of me. Parts of me that just didn't seem to go together. I was a foreigner, to myself, to others. No one knows the real person locked behind these eyes. The mystique that surrounds them is baffling to me also. To many, and at many times, I appear simple, and at other times, I am extremely complex. Frequently, I am described as a loner. Commonly, I am described as strange.

The key to myself is simple: no one, regardless who, finds it easy to decipher this enigma. I was in this world, but not actually of this world. Intelligent, articulate, perceptive, creative—perhaps too creative. It wasn't that I was a loner because I didn't consider myself as an acting member of life. Instead, I created my own world. A world so safe and detached, I formed different images to function for me. They were the other me's, representative of specific ages and events throughout my life. They came to be my companions: the ones I battled with cognitively; the ones that became my silent confidantes; the ones who often conflicted my thinking to the point of suicide and then struggled to save me from myself; the ones who cried when my own system shut down; the ones who, somehow, experienced the pain, the anger, the joy; the ones who battled all the emotions safely sealed until the time for their release. Time is not steadfast for anyone. However, the event, the emotion was captured in total oblivion by the mind for storage until it could begin its labored processing.

The pain, the energy exerted in the effort to understand the horror of my early escapings became obstacles to living—no happiness, no security, no family, no hope. The safe tucking of the hurt neatly within the separate me's allowed survival. How strange the mind works when confrontations of death arise to instill that struggle against death, especially if that one event would bring an end to the painful devastation. That instinctive fueling of an exasperating situation supporting the perpetrators utilizing an innocent child as their ploy.

Fairness in life seemed absent, or just a myth. Was life a myth? Or was there logic to be found somewhere within all the madness? If it was there, one of the other me's would find it at some point while I remained divided and lost among the splittings of my core.

Infrequently, very infrequently, I was almost a whole, able to keep my thoughts together without that sense of fragmentation. Those times were so few and for such short periods of time that fewer and fewer persons were able to recognize me as a person, preferring to describe me as strange. And I was strange, never adapting to the world, because I chose to withdraw into a personal world of my creation. A safer world where questions, pain, and abuse never occurred. A world in which no one ever had the opportunity to touch me, to scream at me, to look at me.

During the hours in which no one would come upstairs, the hunger pains would set in; and then the sleep would follow, which generated the plunderings of the young mind. Plunderings which evoked the small sense of logic she and the other me's were able to assimilate. With no one to offer help, it was the only recourse available to the young victim. The shared thoughts became the experiential background upon which each of the splittings would base their particular personality. Personalities that prohibited the integration of them all within the core, which would later provide problematic avenue after avenue as the bends of life were approached. It was the inability to approach these bends with an integrated self that prolonged and compounded the already present splittings of the core. They made life manageable for the moment; the future just simply did not exist.

Retrospectively, there was no future, only the repetition of the present, forever frozen in time, awaiting the transgressions of hate, demise, lust, and power. The uncontrollable odds were stacked ever so increasingly high against the product of the tyrant and the beast. Oh, how long time must feel when stagnated before the flames of the transgression release their unbearable heat.

But those thoughts were far from the mind of the little toddler, lost for now in a dreamland where the coldness and hatred of the room were replaced with lovely scented flowers brought to her by a secret friend. He was a little spider monkey named Lyles, whose long, skinny arms gently embraced the weeping child, delicately rubbing his long slender fingers back and forth. Brushing the wet curls from her face, his long tail swished just a fraction before curling around and resting in the palm of the hand free to grasp it close.

It was then, and only then, that she was free to plunk the remaining thumb inside her mouth. Without thought, the index finger curled around the nose end, securely locking all in place. There it would stay as Lyles and the other me's shared with her in a tea party, served elegantly on a white lace tablecloth with a small pink rose and baby's breath in a crystal vase, petite china cups, and white linen napkins. Lyles carefully poured tea from the teapot, and with a word of caution, invited the other me's to partake. It was most beautiful watching Lyles and the other me's sharing more than just a cup of tea. They shared love and friendship. They were a family so far removed from the tyrant that no harm would ever beset them. It was important to keep them from harm.

CHAPTER 4

No longer did the tyrant dunk my head into the toilet; but no longer did I suck my thumb—at least not in her presence. Things were changing rapidly. The tyrant was gone for long periods of time; in her place, was another, unknown lady. She brought my meals to me, bathed me, and dressed me. Each night just before leaving, the strange lady put me to bed, without a story and without a good-night song. Once she tried to give me a kiss, but I pulled away. I wanted no kisses, and exchanged few words with this stranger who would soon depart. With her departure came the return of the tyrant. To avoid her, I made a world without her, much like my invisible shelf. Sitting quietly outside her reach, I could see the world from which I was detached and safe, where observations were free and bountiful.

The watchful eyes of the tyrant were forever scrutinizing the movement of this young child. Never interacting, just watching, sternly watching. The child simply endured. Attempts at involving the tyrant only provoked angry aggressions—throwing her doll over the veranda minutes after striking her with it; giving her soapy water when she asked for a drink; withholding meals because it was inconvenient for her; waving a knife in her face, shouting how she would cut out her bladder if she wet on herself; reminding her how ugly she was, and if she made a sound or even a whimper, she could make her uglier; the name she gave her—"the ugly child." Screams for her to go away when the men arrived.

These were the things which prefaced a walk for the "ugly child" into her separate world.

A beautiful world where she was not the ugly child, but had long curls tied back with pink satin bows, embellishing her pink and white balloon dress, pink socks, and white shoes. She was adorned with a smile. Happy and safe, she found she could live here in this world. All talking, whimpering, struggling subsided, creating a world too inviting to leave or share. It was *her* world completely sealed with no escapings, no intruding unless she allowed it. Here life could be pleasant and fun. There she chose to stay. Communication ceased with the exception of the eyes. The tyrant conveyed much through her eyes, always attempting to destroy or worse, mutilate beyond repair.

The one she perceived to be so ugly left her hatred outside of the bubble. Inside the bubble, covered in plastic, the small three-year-old did not feel pain. The plastic sealed so easily, she could accept meals by pulling them through—power that only she possessed. Toys could be retrieved in the same manner, but never could another person break through. Many strangers tried to suction her out and into their world, but they failed.

She used this bubbled world for many many months, talking within her mind, but forever quiet to others. She truly loved being separate and detached from them; besides, no one really cared. In the bubble, someone did care, another me, frozen in time until it would be safe to release her.

The world made family life rigid, cold, withdrawn. That's when Nanna came. The tyrant was away again, perhaps battering some other child. Nanna was happy and sang a lot. Always she sat with her while she ate, unaware that the meal and the child were inside her bubbled world. Her smiles were new to the child, something she had seen all too infrequently. That same smile was there at bedtime, when always she read a story or two, kissed her good night, and tucked her in to remain safely until morning's awakening.

Nanna's consistent loving care was viewed from the bubble while waiting for her to scream relentlessly; throw away toys and books; to put needles under her nails; to put spoonfuls of salt on her tongue; to put chunks of ice in her bath; to make her sleep standing up, striking her each time she fell; dunking her head into the toilet. Never did Nanna do any of these things, always being patient as she waited for an invitation into the child's world.

Months and months passed before the first small step was taken that began the acceptance of Nanna. First with a smile, then with silent interactions and pressure from no one, the child slowly saw the difference in Nanna and the tyrant. Just as slowly, Nanna gently moved herself closer to the bubbled world. It wasn't that Nanna wanted to step inside that world, but rather, she wanted the child to step outside. The stepping out could be temporary or permanent. If she chose to return, she could. The importance was that she step out of her world, thus creating a slight chance she may decide to stay. It was a bright, sunny day when she chose to trust Nanna enough to step out of her bubbled world, risking her survival. She was curious about Nanna, maybe even hopeful. Above all, Nanna was not intrusive.

The stay outside of her world was short. She wasn't quite comfortable waiting for the pain to start. And when it did not, she retreated back inside her bubbled world. Nanna seemed to understand her departure, for within that world, she could roll and roll until her world and she were far, far away.

That was her security time after time during the course of the next several months as a small bridge of trust was formed. Its construction spanned all channels as one stranger struggled with a smaller stranger, instilling by some minute gesture a miraculous breath of hope. A breath to be repeated over and over, allowing expansion and change. And with the passage of time, that repeated breath birthed the hope allowing her to venture out of the bubbled world on a regular basis; it also allowed her to grasp the bubble when her need for escape swelled beyond containment.

Initially, there were many times when she needed to escape, *always* with Nanna's approval. The trips away became less in frequency and duration until one day there were no more escapes when Nanna was present. There were even times when laughter filled the nursery. She remembers that vividly, for once the laughter escalated, capturing her parents' attention and presence; and suddenly, there was a great need for flight, for escape into the bubbled world that kept her safe.

Their presence and their attacks created the retreat, growing in duration and frequency until just the thought of them taking her from Nanna provoked an early and swift escape—these escapes would continue for decades of a troubled life. Perhaps it was then she first recognized her use of the bubbled world. It was her escape from them—her parents—which caused the splittings. Running away from them psychologically was all the running this little one could do. There was no need to run from Nanna, for she had convinced her to stop her escapings. With Nanna present, the air felt comfortable and clean, easy to breath and warm. The nursery was a nice place to live, not one that she wanted to leave; and if wishes could come true, she would never have to be without this.

But she was to learn all too soon that her wish would not be granted, that her bubbled world of plastic was actually the safety net of her own creation when her parents failed. And it was a very good creation, making survival of a horrific situation possible. It also made escape into that world all too desirable when life became unbearable. It was a safe world, but also an unrealistic one, in that perfection and purity filled her bubble, staging a barrier that would not be when she once again ventured out into the real world.

CHAPTER 5

Thinking, thinking, thinking . . . the longer she thought, the more she remembered. More of the things she had perceived as mere thoughts of horror were actually crimes of violence. There had been safe, happy times, but then, there were the times in the parks when he made her sting and bleed.

It was Nanna I thought about as I scrambled into the bubble, turning to watch as he packed the soil and leaves around the other me. The hole was so deep that only her head protruded out into the air. He looked angrily at her, gritting and grinding his teeth as he glared into her face. The anger was evident—a face so filled with hatred. She was frightened of him. That's why it was nice to think of Nanna and how she promised to take care of her. Soon she would find her, get her out, and clean away the debris.

She always saved her. She thought of how good she would feel when the warm waters of the tub washed away the filth plastered upon her by him; the softness of Nanna's arms caressing as she gently dried away the pain; and the story she would tell about the little girl she loved very, very much who lived an unhappy life, but that soon she would be able to change all of that, bringing the little girl to live ever after with her in a small cottage far, far away in "Nanna Land." It was easy to sleep then—the child, her blankie, and Nanna all together in the sealed bubble.

Suddenly, the flailing of his hand against her cheek focused her mind upon him once again. The stinging brought tears to her eyes, but the frightened creature blinked and blinked, fighting to keep them from running down her soiled spotted cheeks. He would hit her again if she cried. She remembered him telling her many times that crying was bad and would cause horrible things to happen to her, like parts of her body being cut away and hung upon the tree branches as feedings for the large black crows. Whenever the tears started forming in his presence, the beaks of the crows could be felt piercing through the skin, ripping away the tissue and vessels until their thirst for food was quenched. Again her mind escaped into the bubble, away from the actions at hand, perhaps to avoid his near-fatal moves or just a simple attempt at pretending she did not exist.

Grabbing her chin, he methodically described the packing of the debris, heavily laden with worms and water to ensure her stillness, and how the worms would embed within the body should any movement be detected before his return. She stood very, very still, yearning to be removed, wanting to get out, to be clean. From time to time, the worms nibbled at her skin igniting movement, but nothing would move under all the weight. She was glued to the soil as he mounted newspapers over her head, making her oblivious to the warmth and light of the sun, obscuring her presence from passersby, should there be any.

Abruptly, the papers came off, but he was still there. Taking a roll of tape from his pocket, he moved to the back of her, out of sight. Without a word, the tape was slapped across her mouth, forcing her silence, but not her screams for they were heard louder and louder within her mind and within the mind of the one inside the bubble. Life is often cruel, and seldom does it care enough to issue even the slightest warning. Instead, it demands that one give and give, for the battle between life and self always yields life as victorious when the self finally succumbs to its stress. And she had succumbed to life, existing within the trap of having been born into a situation where the most hideous of crimes prevailed.

The screams of horror within her mind continued with the newspaper mound closing out the warmth and light once again. But this time, he appeared to have placed stones around the edges, disallowing any clue to its secrecy below. She was alone in the mud-filled hole for just a short time, when her mind summoned that other me, the clean, four-year-old little girl who would not have had the dirty, dirty debris clinging to her dress, the one who had not been hurt by him, the one who could be loved and cuddled and wanted by someone.

She placed her inside the bubble and sealed it out of reach, protecting her from the touches, the screams, the blood. And there she would stay with me until it was safe to get down and go home with Nanna. Without the sharing of a word, she would put her to rest inside her mind, sometimes for days, but other times, just for the night. She appeared at those times to be a doll rather than herself. That way she would be inaccessible to his touches and evil words, undesirable to his lustful passion. There would be no feelings, no desires, no hatred, just the eternal hours of solitude and eternally lost in another world. But for now, she was in the mud and worm-filled hole, waiting for his return. At least *he* wasn't hurting her at the present time—the mud and worms prevented that.

Until his return, she would remain in this grave. It felt like a long, long time—perhaps hours—giving her time to think, to grasp his anger. Telling Nanna was what had gotten her in this hole. If she had just not said anything, he would not have buried her. It wasn't any of Nanna's business—he had said so. Nanna was paid to do as he said, and if she could not, she would leave. She wanted Nanna to stay, but she asked her why she was bleeding, while holding herself. Nanna was angry when she told her daddy had hurt her, but it would be better soon. It was an accident, and talking about it would make him feel sad. How this mournful creature wanted Nanna to be quiet, but she kept asking questions and getting upset.

When Daddy came back, she was still talking about it, making him angry. He was frightening the way he screamed. Nanna cried and cried as she rocked the little child, holding her tenderly. If only Nanna had been quiet, she wouldn't be in this hole packed with mud and worms. She would be able to breathe instead of being stuffed under the smelly newspapers. Their odor was quite different from others—not as strong as a wet dog, but not as weak as flowers in early bloom—much like bay leaves, which at first capture the nostrils, surround them, and then stifle with no escape.

It was scary to think of what he had done to force her to keep silent. It would seem more right if we would talk about the hurt. If she said anything, he would put her in this same hole again, only then he would put her head all the way under. There would be no breathing, especially after the mud and worms merged into her mouth. Her nostrils would be filled quickly; and the eyelids, laden with the mixture, bound shut as if stitched together. Her mind would want to burst her body apart, gasping for air, a cleansing breath blowing away all tracings of him.

The pain had returned. The burning, stinging sensation making her want to move, to hold herself, to scream. The damp, packed earth prevented her movement. She was immobilized, changeable only by his return. The stinging had stopped, but she needed to urinate more, since she had discontinued when the stinging began. It was going to sting again, but she had to go. She just could not wait any longer. Tears flowed down her cheeks as the stinging radiated deep within, leaving shooting pain after shooting pain. She thought of the trails amidst her soiled cheeks from the tears she had shed, but she needed to cry. Nanna had said crying was a way of laundering feelings. And as she cried, she realized that there would be no one to dry away her tears and no one to make the stinging subside. She wondered why no one ever told her about daddies and this, and why this was all right to do when it hurt so bad.

In the distance, ducks were quacking, but it was all dark for her. The warmth of the sun was gone along with its light, both too weak to infiltrate his barrier of hate. Her legs hurt from the pushing and pulling earlier. Her ears rang with the remnants of his cruel laugh. Muscles twitched from the piercing of himself against her bottom; his hand held high and the thundering of his palm against her head; the sudden gouging of his fingers inside of her as he covered her mouth with the other hand, muffling her scream; the pebble that pressed heavily into her back. Somehow, she needed all these thoughts to disperse.

It was the blood that scared her most as it ran down her legs and across her ankles. It hurt to move, but it hurt to stand still, also. Hopping from one foot to the other, she held herself, only to have him slap her until she stood quietly. Her white lace panties were becoming soiled with blood as he screamed at her to put them on. Tears ran down her cheeks as warning after warning was issued not to tell anyone about the game they had played. A game she would replay many times within her memory, reexperiencing each thread of pain. Memories of eternity with no diminishment perceived.

Oh, how she wished Nanna had remained silent or that Daddy had cleaned the blood away before going home. She would not be in this hole now if only . . . This was where she would remain . . . maybe forever. It was hard to breathe; she longed for fresh air. Internally, she screamed! Externally, she silenced her cry. And within her mind, she envied the four-year-old dressed in clean clothing with no trace of tears upon her cheeks. This was the me she yearned for, sensing that somewhere she could be her when the time was right.

She quickly and quietly put her to rest, turning her mind to the other me stuck within this dirty grave. She dressed the poor child in a black, soiled, and tattered dress, giving her a knife to protect herself from the beast. Protection was necessary, especially with ones so young. This had become a strategy game of who could control and how much. This four-year-old, dressed in black, was instructed not to allow her death by his hands, regardless of what he attempted. Death was the goal of this other me. Therefore, she was prepared to follow that path without interruption by the beast. Never, never would he kill her, for she had been programmed to do that herself, thus disallowing his satisfaction of having that ultimate control. That was the reasoning behind the knife—protection from him and death from herself.

CHAPTER 6

Suddenly, the abuse came to a dramatic halt—no more terror, no more pain, no more hatred. The chilling laughs disappeared. More time was spent with me, but it wasn't like before. They were now concerned about my health, my heart. The sickness that ensued confined me to bed for several years, during which I was the focus of their attention. Those were the times when I had begun to think it was my mind that was bad, just thinking horrid thoughts about my parents. It would have been impossible for any parent to have done what my mind was telling me. I was sure of that, because now they acted as though they loved me; they took care of me; and always, they left me with Nanna instead of taking me to the places where they had hurt me. I was ready to believe it was all over. Month after month, they continued to be kind to me, forcing my mind to form question after question as to why I thought these horrible things, why I felt so fragmented.

There were actually nights when my dreams were loving, desirable, safe. Dreams greatly enjoyed by the affective me until locating the cognitive me that sifted the disturbances between how I felt and what had happened earlier. It was one of those lovely dreams I was just coming out of when my eyes fell upon my father sitting quietly in a chair by my bed. Trying to adjust to awakening, I simply awaited the full wakefulness of myself. Upon his lap sat a beautiful white rabbit with a pink satin bow about his neck; his pink eyes stared back at me as I attempted to discern if what I saw was actually there. It was the wriggling of his nose as he twitched and twitched that brought a realness to the scene. It was Easter morning, I was still ill, and staying in bed had become unbearable. Looking at the rabbit, I sensed goodness, warmth, something that was just mine, never to be taken away.

My father saw the delight the rabbit had created and quickly slipped it under the covers where the rabbit and I could snuggle softly in the morning sun's rays. He was mine—soft, warm, loving. He would not turn on me, making me his victim as they had done. There was no way he could hurt me. At long last, there was someone with whom to share my thoughts other than the different me's. Mr. Rabbit and I became inseparable, as my heart perceived him to be my best friend.

As the days passed, the tyrant began to emerge once again. She hated Mr. Rabbit, striking him many times in my presence, making me cry, which provoked her relentless screams. Perhaps it was me she wanted to strike, for the fury, vivid within her eyes, was always directed at me. She knew the rabbit was my only friend. Several times she had rushed at me with her fists held high, stopping short of my head, only to grab Mr. Rabbit and throw him heavily upon the floor. His hind leg was injured one day when she threw him against the wall. When Daddy came home, she told him *I* had been cruel to Mr. Rabbit. And, later that afternoon, Mr. Rabbit went to live outside in a specially made cage. I wondered then if the tyrant would be striking me next.

The fear I felt was all too familiar. I searched for the bubble but couldn't find it this time. Instead, I found a door leading away from the room. Passing through the door, an angel was seated on a bench under a tree and beckoned me to join her. She wanted to share with me a beautiful land far away. Watching intensely, I saw myself running through a field, wind-blown curls bouncing freely in a raven-tinted mass, like the long branches of the weeping willow during the early spring breeze. The ribbon of white satin flowed as if drawn by the warmth of the love placed within each curl. She moved in slow motion as she ran across the field high with wild flowers adorned by butterflies quietly leaving when the small hand plucked the flower from its root, unknowingly shortening its life, to join the others securely clasped within the other hand. From flower to flower, with smiles and giggles, this other me was in a dreamland, where there were no wrongdoings, where clouds floated gracefully down upon her, engulfing her shoulders, her eyes lifting upward to the blue-filled sky. The clouds were pillows of love, so soft, so warm, so tender, so important to hold onto, even when the sun was set and the clouds mere shadows in the moon. Looking over her shoulder, she saw the love of her angel, knowing someday she would share that with someone she loved.

Oh, how beautiful she felt as she lay back onto the grass among the flowers. Closing her eyes, their fragrances filled her head, exploding with joy, with safety. She could stay forever in this field, gathering small, wild relics of perfection reflecting the goodness of elements working together cohesively without the friction of the evil. Alone, happy, energized, alive—oh, how different life was for this bundle of purity—clean, fresh, loved, wanted.

Laughing and frolicking among the summer blooms sprinkled with butterflies, she glanced slowly back at the tyrant, who was trying to terrorize one of the me's, smiled and breathed quietly, knowing she did not have the power to penetrate her world of safety. The ribbons flowed and the curls bounced as she freely ran and ran and ran. . . It was easy to run, easy to breathe, easy to be lost within this solitude of peace.

And it was the peace she valued more than the freedom. Control with peace was acceptable . . . perhaps acceptable because free peace appeared to be an impossibility. Whichever, she yearned to live it all over and over, refusing to release her newly discovered tranquility. There was a need to absorb it all, much like the sun-scorched earth swallows up the long-awaited rains. An endless absorption, quenching a thirst bigger than the universe.

For the present, no one existed. The entire universe was alone and away from this world. None of the disgusting smells of them; of their games of fun; of their crimes of passion; of their needs to destroy. Ingrained in her memory forever, however long her escape into this paradise would be, were the flowers swaying in the gentle breeze, standing high above the green grass mesmerized by a fragrance so unique it dazzled the butterflies and set forth a hypnosis among the bumblebees only visible in minute images of the slow flashes.

Her running and laughing began to slow, taking longer and longer for the images and aroma to tantalize her senses, not in a labored manner, but rather in the visuals as she, too, had become totally mesmerized by the intensity. It was an omen for rest, for sleep, for an extended nap, allowing the skin's absorption. Osmosis! Total submission to the pleasures at hand until the mind allowed sleep inside her new found paradise. Slowly and softly, her eyelids relaxed, forbidding the infiltration of the lovely sun. Its warmth nurturing the body and mind, preparing it for its return to the world of others. It was the final enjoyment as all cells about the body could, at last, fall prey to rest, a welcomed rest, but also, a very hard-earned rest. A rest to restore the lost energy, to regroup, to become distant, and yes, to escape the travesties of her being.

This sleep was unique, always unique. It was her bridge back into the real world, birthing conflict, in that this was the return to the much-dreaded terror, yet a bridge which invited its crossing relentlessly for the tranquility of sleep. The body could no longer resist as the mind envied the peace. Always a price to pay, maybe not understood in its concept, but certainly understood in reality. For now, it was safe. It formed an escape.

Sleep, deep sleep, made the crossing of the bridge a retreat—a temporary retreat. The crossing was lengthy, disallowing disturbances and creating a constant flowing state of sleep. The entire universe was void and silent in preparation for her transition. Breaching the space between each slat of wood was as if stepping upon a cloud moving from bridge to bridge, paradise to paradise. Her legs seemed too short to breach the spaces, where the angels minimized her deficits, carrying her from step to step. The incline of the bridge was marked with degrees, as if representatives of different levels in her sleep. Each to be acknowledged; none to be ignored. Each allowing passage onto the next with no turning back. Departure from one to another also promised the diminishment of a delightful journey.

Again, she looked back at the other me to find the tyrant had closed her hands around her throat, choking her as her screaming reached its peak. Relieved of that pain, her head tilted toward the sky. There would be no need to look back anymore until the bridge was nearly crossed. Her journey and her sleep would be close to finish then; and when her mind was ready, it would allow the demise of this paradise after the other me's return.

Her legs were tired, but the end of the bridge was in

sight. The mind recognized this, making time to look once again at the other me. With courage and obligation, she scanned the distance she had covered. The other me was no longer at a far, far distance, but rather, close behind, and the beautiful field of flowers present only to the front of her. It would soon be time to join her, but first, the pain and her inflictor must be stilled, quieted, preventing the body and mind from hurting.

That is what she was running away from, if she could get away from the other me, then she could escape the pain, replacing it with joy. The first of the other me's high-pitched screams came blasting through. It was time! The paradise was ending. Soon . . . the abrupt end to her world would be here. One last glance over her shoulder showed the other me free from restraint, saddened, and relieved to be going back to her, for it was time to rest briefly.

Life would be at a slower pace for a short while, gradually regaining speed until once again the tormented racing of the mind would cease. This was "catch up" time—a time when nothing really happened good or bad—a brief time allowing the mind and the other me's to become somewhat docile, awaiting the onset of the now dormant variables. This was peace to a degree, but certainly far from contentment. It was just a nonpressured time to be passed in preparation. The other me's were taking naps, long, long naps. The child was simply housing them in her mind, not to be disturbed until the rumblings of the other me's alerted her.

At times, it was for a couple of weeks. Other times, just a few days. It wasn't the duration of time which affected the suffering, for too many other variables controlled that element. It occurred frequently and somehow fueled the internal will to survive. Or perhaps it was just the intensity of the paradise that made the suffering by the other me's durable. It certainly relieved the guilt she bestowed upon herself for abandoning the other me's to become recipients of the tremendous pain.

CHAPTER 7

For many months, the images of the clean four-year-old and the beautiful experience of the seven-year-old with the angels clustered about her mind contradicted reality. Softly, she pushed them back, avoiding the pain that their loveliness instilled. The depression of this child was in one of its depths presently; perhaps because the contrast in what was and what should have been was more real, more understood. The conflict presented was much too great for her to endure.

The bubble, used almost always, was appearing hopeless. Not hopeless in sustaining her, but hopeless in that it offered no possibility of the life she desired, no chance of the paradise shown briefly to her by the angels and once by her own mind. This may have been the beginning of anger in her, for many thoughts of destruction seethed below her surface, which at times made her not search for the bubble, but rather to yearn for one of them to kill her, to destroy her if she could not have the joy she had glimpses of earlier.

Times occurred when she pushed the tyrant to kill her, but never would she go that far. Always she stopped short of ending the terror forever, leaving the bewilderment and resentment within this child escalating beyond containment. There just seemed to be something wrong, something missing, when there was this much sadness in a young life. Wondering if this was what life really was, or was going to be, she called for the other me's within her mind to reevaluate their functions. Careful watch of each and their respective roles was a clear indicator of what distressed her core. The me's had all worked to assure the child of survival, but in so doing, two of them had created yearnings for a much better life.

The two-year-old and the four-year-old, dressed in black, were acceptable because they led the same horrible life that she knew. Even the three-year-old was acceptable, since she had found her use time after time. But, she had difficulties with the clean four-year-old and the seven-year-old who had seen the angels. Part of her wanted the angels to rescue her and keep her safe, but they never came, and she wondered if maybe they just shared what heaven would be like or maybe even her life some day. The hope that this angelic paradise could somehow be waiting in the wings for her in the future allowed that other me to stay. But, the four-year-old who was clean, who had not been violated, and who could be loved would have to go far, far away, for she tugged at the child's heartstrings, almost maliciously reinforcing the realization she could never be any of the things represented by this other me.

The mind of the child could no longer endure what she had missed out on because of her parents. It was cruel for this other me to taunt her, to make her cry, to sadden her with thoughts that could never be. It was this me that was always so clean, so proper, so sure of who she was and where she was going. One that, to this child, could only exist in a land with the angels, where wicked and evil people were unknown. The child loved this clean four-year-old, wanting to be like her, to be free of all the filth and terror, but she remembered the days spent at the parks, when he tore away at her flesh leaving her bloody and hurting.

Emotions were hard for this child to accommodate, but she knew more than ever that she was jealous of this other me, for never would she be able to forget the debris from the park, pain from his lust, and her intense yearning to live with the angels high above, higher than the black hole in the top of the universe. She placed this other me inside the bubble, sealing it securely, leaving her there for months and months. Many times she joined her there in their haven, where she held her hand and shielded her eyes from the terrors that had created them all. It was comforting for her to stay there inside the child's bubbled world initially, but then the simple nature of the child allowed the jealousy to rise, forcing the removal of the other me from the bubble.

This was a contained jealousy, for no harsh words or quick movements or glaring looks were exchanged as the young child searched for a place to store the other me where she would be safe. There was no need to harm the other me, just a need to get her out of the way until the pain of what she was could subside. With tenderness the child had never known, she cradled this other me against her heart, loving her and imagining the fresh smells of a four-year-old as she extended her departure.

She first thought of putting her inside her heart, but feared her mind would not keep her safe. There was much doubt that if she placed the other me in her heart, the day may come when she would savagely attack her out of jealousy, just as they had her out of hatred and lust. So she did the only thing she could do; she placed her securely inside the heart of the seven-year-old who had visited heaven. She would be safe there away from the jealous child should rage overtake her, thus allowing danger to come to the clean four-year-old.

From what the jealousy stemmed wasn't purely evident, but it appeared this child was overwhelmed because this duplicate had the chance she did not; had a childhood, hers having been viciously stolen away; had cleanness, which she would never have; had little girl thoughts, which she had but were tainted with adult lust. She was the other me who had escaped the terror and pain; who could laugh, sing, smile; who looked at the stars and dreamt; who looked at nature and saw wonder; and who *never* hoped to be suctioned beyond that black hole in the universe where no one knew if life existed, but where nothing could be as bad as life down here.

This was, in a sense, a burial for this other me. For the child, it was almost an emancipation from one of the many strings that seemed to forever weigh her down. Whether this was the best solution to the jealousy or not wasn't the issue. The issue was survival. Not only survival of this child, but also of this other me who was just as innocent as the violated child. Using this option prevented this vulnerable child from becoming a perpetrator.

CHAPTER 8

My mind appeared to have a self-protecting quality as it searched its crevices and folds for reasoning to justify its actions. There must have been some warning signs along the way that I just simply missed. My "why" search was intense as my mind tried to focus in on any act or statement that should have issued warning, but didn't. Suddenly life was filled with fear and hatred all over again. My thinking drifted back to that one time when I had experienced this precise feeling. The sounds and smells of that time swept through my head. It seemed to have just happened a few hours ago.

There had been a shipment of some kind; and, being nine years old, I went down to the basement to inspect it. A coffin was there in one corner. Shocked, I asked, "Why?"

Looking at me, my father said, "It's to be used at the haunted house. It just arrived early."

It resided there in the basement for months and months untouched, with its cold, cold affect. Suddenly, one afternoon, my father sent me down to retrieve an item from the basement. I looked at the coffin, flattening myself against the opposite wall. Locating the requested item with my eyes, my heart pounded loudly. My chest felt crushed. I would have to walk too close to the coffin. Timidly, I took very small steps in that direction. With my intense thoughts, his arrival behind me went unnoticed until his wicked laugh blasted my hearing. As I whirled around in fright, he lunged for me.

Running from the basement, I frantically searched for

Nanna so her arms and words could comfort me. She always did, despite my father's power. Always, she voiced her unhappiness to him. She soothed my fears and dried my tears with love and kindness. And, then, she and I sat in the sun, making shapes among the clouds. Retrospectively, she tempered the evilness of my parents, and would have been the one to save me from them had she still been employed.

The coffin was moved out for Halloween; I breathed a big sigh of relief. Its return several days later brought back that familiar fear.

I asked, "How long will it be staying?"

My father replied, "It will always be here with us."

My fear asked why, only to hear his chilled reply, "Every man needs a coffin around."

At that time, I did not understand his intentions. There was a mystery about him and the manner in which he responded to people, as if always with an in-depth strategy working within his mind of utmost importance, unperceivable to all others. Avoidance was my best strategy. I would not think about it. I would not look at it.

Numerous times my father had taken me down to look at the coffin during its eternal nights of stay. One particular evening, I sensed danger as he instructed me to accompany him once again.

Standing by the death-evoking coffin, he asked, "How long do you think someone could live with the lid closed?" Without answering, I stepped back, shaking. He opened the lid, pulling me close. His laughing and pulling forced me to scream. He allowed me to pull away as I made my safe exit to my Nanna. She promised to always protect me and I believed she would. Carefully and very lovingly, she put me to bed, rubbing my back until I fell asleep. She always knew just the right moment to reach down and give me a kiss, so the last thought my mind captured was her love.

Morning brought great sadness. My Nanna was gone. No good-bye, no anything. She and her things were gone. I asked my father where she had gone. He just said, "She won't be back."

I've always wondered what happened to her. I knew she would never leave without a good-bye to me. She loved me unconditionally. At first, I thought she had just gone for the holidays, but when she was still gone at Christmas, my hopes died. I knew she wouldn't ever be back.

Later, I was able to understand her dismissal. It was just before the rapings. He had already made his plans—she would only interfere. It was imperative to the success of his plan that she be dismissed. I think of her often, especially when the memories of the coffin flash back. By supposition, she and I sensed danger from the coffin and my father well in advance.

The coffin had remained there for years. Never did he use it to frighten me again, until one May. It was Mother's Day weekend and I was home alone with him. I grieved silently for the Nanna that had been gone so very, very long. I missed her always. I was overwhelmed by all the particulars of my life. The confusion and lack of love was slowly destroying me with each passing day. No one seemed to care about me. I had no hope. The weekend was his and we were always alone.

The events had molded me into a silent, frightened being. He came to me demanding sex. I was silent again on this night. I hated these times with him. His lust so prevalent and repulsive, my flesh became prickly at the thought. As I watched him undress, I prayed he would die. His erect penis in my face was repugnant. The sinful looks he cast my way were alarming. He should not be doing this to me! It was wrong and I hated him! Moving his hands across my chest, he moaned, slipping them inside my clothing and throwing them onto the floor. Pushing and moaning, he moved his body on top of me. And then the abrupt ending.

Looking at me, he said, "I want to hear it from you. Tell me what you want!" I remained silent.

He continued, "You're a fucking whore! I told you to tell me!"

I said, "I don't want you to do that to me."

Slapping me, he said, "I'll fuck you when I want to, and I want to now!"

Jumping off the bed, I slipped my robe on as I ran toward the door. He shoved me into the wall, clasping his hands around my neck. Grinding his teeth, he threatened, "I'm going to kill you, bitch!"

The terror had begun. Throwing me in the direction of the stairs, he screamed for me to die. Tumbling down the stairs, I hoped I could somehow get away. Running after me, he screamed for me to get into the basement. I knew he would kill me this time, for he had never been this angry.

My death was imminent. I ran down the stairs and into the basement toward an exit. Grabbing my long hair, he pulled me toward him. Turning my head toward him, he spat in my face. Laughing, he pushed me toward the coffin. It was getting closer and closer and closer! Would he kill me and then put my body in the coffin? My mind was racing! Yes! He would kill me first, before he put me into the coffin. We were there! Directly in front of me was the coffin. As he raised the lid, I was horrified. Screaming and pleading, I sat down. He pulled me up from the floor glaring into my face.

I pleaded, "Kill me first, please!"

Laughing, he said, "It won't take long for you to die once I close the lid."

I stared at the open coffin.

Squeezing my face, he sternly said, "All you had to do was tell me what you wanted and we wouldn't be here. I'm going to put you in there to suffocate. Then I'll fuck you till you rot!" I was so terrified.

Suddenly, I found myself sitting upon a shelf, looking sadly at the scene below.

He picked her up and forced her into the coffin. She fought, trying to get out, but he pushed her down as he closed the lid. She saw it falling toward her, screaming only to hear her screams become muffled as he closed the lid. It was cold and dark. She couldn't see, couldn't breathe, her chest hurt. She was dying! And she would be alone while it happened, in a closed-in place with no light.

I felt something. It was cold against my face. I heard sounds as the dampness of my clothing soaked into the flesh. I opened my eyes and saw light. The lid was open, but I didn't feel like moving. I felt sick, dizzy, unable to move. I must have had a nightmare, but it seemed too real. Time would tell for sure. But for now, my mind needed sleep.

I had been awake for a while when I looked at the clock, a quarter past three. The house was silent. Suddenly and quietly, he appeared at my door. I still felt different, not sure of much, but definitely fearful.

Walking over to my bed, he calmly and sternly said, "I let you live tonight, but next time you don't do as I say, I'll put you back in there and let you die!" I remained silent.

He had just confirmed it was not a nightmare—it really happened. And now, on those frightening nights as the deadly storms blow through, I relive that over and over. I fall asleep many times and awaken to find my heart racing, my chest hurting, and my clothing damp from his terror.

That was a long time ago, but it was the same feeling, the same fear, the same shock as now. Was that in preparation for the rape or was he, psychologically, a demented soul? Never had I been so frightened as that night, when all the light was shut out and I was alone inside his coffin.

I'm not sure if I think he was kinder by letting me live or if it would have been better to have just let me die that night. If his intent was to intimidate me into never refusing his orders, he had succeeded. I think a part of me died that night; or perhaps, I just visited hell momentarily.

CHAPTER 9

It's almost Christmas Eve again. How I hate that night so embossed upon my burdensome memory, never forgetting the cruel and devastating scars he inflicted. Never even a fading of those minute details which appear almost humane when compared with other "special" nights.

He professed his lustful acts as natural teachings a father must provide for his daughter's sexual preparation. The nature of his violations were unlimited, forcing me to wish many times for my death. Countless nights I wanted to kill him. The frustration was more than I could endure. In his presence, he would terrorize me. And in his absence, his memories would take over, with the holidays bringing the most painful to surface.

Frequently, he was dominant in my dreams, in my thoughts, and in my destructive desires. I was his prisoner and he was my warden. He controlled every aspect of me and my life. With his control and preparation, he had ruined and destroyed every element of life in me. I feared his threats of "no other man desiring me" would actualize.

His memory plagues my soul, grasping tighter and stronger until even the ringing of the phone creates fearful illusions of his voice laughing back at the product of his sadistic mind. I wait in morbid fear of the day his voice comes blasting through the phone, shrieking those horrid and repulsive whisperings of so long, long ago. These thoughts provoke that "little girl fear" all too familiar to my memory.

The fear of enduring shocking and painful hours of torment, and also, the fear of death.

He played upon my fears, terrorizing me to the satisfaction of his lustful self. It had been months since the snakes, but it was as fresh in my memory as this morning's sunrise. Oh, how I hated his snakes! Just that vision told me what he wanted. His glaring face sent chilling messages not to be ignored. I only knew the creation of an adversarial position meant more pain and horror for me. His desire of my verbal participation in his sinful lust was not fulfilled. It was that denial that commenced the painful attacks.

For six days, he walked around the pool, dropping one snake per day into the water, never speaking or interacting with me until night closed out the light. The hours of darkness brought his violent rapes and demands to hear me say things I did not feel. My head rocked from side to side with the blows his fists delivered as he screamed for me to beg for his continuance.

Day seven was hell. I knew the number of snakes he had dropped into the pool. I also knew the limit he had set. I walked out to the pool to see them swimming, darting quickly from side to side. My knees hurt, and I felt all weak inside. Horror struck when he slowly walked to the pool's edge with another snake. He looked at me for a long time before walking away. My heart dropped. I had no way of predicting his next move. My only recourse—wait in agonizing terror.

The bright sunlight seemed my haven of safety. Surely, he would not bother me outside. I positioned myself far away from the pool, but where I could watch should he remove the snakes. Several times he came out to the pool without approaching me. And when he did make his approach, he demanded my swimsuit. With my opposition, he ripped it from me. Laughing, he touched my body saying, "I'm going to throw you in with my snakes if I have any problems out of you." As he walked away, he pointed to the snakes, laughing loudly. I sensed my only friend would be the stoppage of time. Nervously, I awaited his return.

My heart pounded swiftly as he walked from the house, keeping his eyes in constant focus on me. Then, for many horribly tormenting minutes, he sat opposite me, watching as I squirmed under his wicked stare.

Unknown to him, I journeyed to my shelf of safety as the fear destroyed my ounce of courage. Looking down, I saw him as he tossed her into the snaky waters. He laughed and laughed, but did nothing to help her. He knew how frightened she was of snakes, but he still didn't help.

Hurrying to the side of the pool, she had visual images of the snakes wrapping around her, touching their scales against her body. She rushed through the water to his outstretched hand. She tried to grasp it, but he pushed her away. He shoved her head under the water, where she could still hear his laughter. With snake-infested water surrounding her, she imagined all his snakes encasing her body. Fearful, she thought he was going to kill her. She was afraid of dying. She wasn't ready to accept death. Suddenly, he pulled her from the pool. She remembered an intense relief from the snaky water; and for the first time in a long, long time, she thought there was good in him. She would be safe once again.

With the same rapid haste that he jerked her from the water, he began his passionate advances on the lawn. Without warning, calmly and unexpectedly, she felt him pull himself off of her. Taking her hand, he walked toward the house. Going up the stairs was indicative of his desires.

Sternly, he asked, "What do you want Daddy to do to his little girl?"

When she failed to respond, he shoved her against the wall. It's hard to remember how many times he slugged away at her. It seemed he expected her to know things she did not. When she attempted to explain this to him, he hit her until she just happened to do whatever it was he desired.

I remember on the stairs that day, he shoved me into the wall, saying, "You had better learn to like doing this with me. I won't let you do it with anybody else."

When I didn't respond to him, he started fondling my breasts. Using his tongue, he indicated parts of my breasts he would "cut off" if I didn't tell him what he wanted to hear. Pushing his body against mine, he laughed as he whispered harshly his intentions. He walked away giving me hope that he was finished for now. Immediately, I scurried up the remaining stairs and into my bedroom, grabbing clothing should he return.

There was no question as to if he would return, but rather, when. He always returned. I wanted so much for him to just die or disappear. Holding in his hand a white canvas bag, he watched me as he walked around the room. Laughter was frequently a part of his presence those days, which seemed to be maximized by the contents of the bag. Again, I sensed its contents were surely destined to torment me.

Silently, he approached the bed looking intently at my body. He patted the canvas bag, creating movement from within, saying, "If my little girl doesn't beg for what Daddy is giving her, I have a little friend that will make her do it."

But, I was safe, high above his reach, knowing the invisible shelf would keep him away. Securely placing the bag on the bed and his lips on her mouth, he pulled her clothing away. Exposing her breasts seemed to arouse him quickly. Moving his mouth to her breasts, he persisted with a repeat of his desires. She refused. He started whispering his actions. When she failed to repeat his statements, his fists returned, striking her over and over.

He pushed his penis into her mouth, shouting, "Suck Daddy's dick, little girl!"

She hated what he was doing. She moved away only to be quickly jerked back within his reach. She begged for him not to hurt her anymore. Squeezing her breasts with his large hands, he softly said, "Daddy won't hurt his little girl if she does as she has been told. If you don't, God would want me to use whatever will make his little girl obey."

He tied her hands and feet. Laughing, he untied the canvas bag, lifting out a large and threatening snake. Placing it on her stomach, he let it slither around, moving closer and closer to her face. She could see its head sticking up with its tongue thrusting back and forth, back and forth, as she screamed and pleaded for him to get the snake off, but he refused.

Still laughing, he watched the snake crawl toward her mouth. She felt its scaly body as its tongue touched her lips. The delight she saw on his face was greater than usual. It is difficult to understand someone deriving pleasure from this, but he did. As abruptly as he put the snake on her, he removed it. His immediate demand was for the sexual comments he loved to hear from her mouth.

He put the snake back into the canvas bag and tied it. For now, this part of her nightmare was over. She breathed a slight relief. His demands continued, but for some reason, her mouth just would not work. She tried to say those words, but no sounds came out. Anger reflected throughout his body. His eyes glowed with vindictiveness as his fists clenched by his sides. Grinding teeth pierced her hearing as his increasing anger became more prevalent, and she would be the one to receive the brunt of it.

The extreme of that anger made her inability to speak much worse. She knew he would be just as offensive as ever. Her thoughts were of the snake as she watched the slight movement of the canvas bag. He also looked that way. Without warning, he removed the snake from the bag and, with the snake in hand, focused his eyes upon her. The thought of the snake being close to her was utterly resentful. With much cruelty, he stood by her restrained body, holding the snake coiling around his arm. Leaning over slightly, he lowered the snake's head closer to her. The movement of the snake as it ventured through the air was frightening. Pleading with him to stop was unsuccessful. With his very cruel demeanor, he reminded her of his demands. Despite her earnest attempts, she could not say them. Much more anger crossed his face as it reddened. How she wished someone would come home and make him stop. She wished that someone would keep her safe. Inwardly, she knew there was no such person. There was no safety.

The mind is a very volatile adornment to the body. So very useful for many things, but also very destructive for others. I wondered how her mind was dealing with this horrible experience. She looked so confused, I wondered if her mind wanted to scream with damage.

But suddenly, she was aware of another scream. It was the beast. For those few seconds, her mind had intensified with her "why" search pushing the visual of the snake away. His scream made her aware of the snake once again. Oh, how I wished her mouth would speak, to form those lustful words he wanted to hear. He was so intent on her utterances, he would do anything to hear them. That was part of his passion being fulfilled. Perhaps that was why he was so cruel at times. Her thinking, jumping from tangent to tangent with in-depth thoughts, lost all track of the present.

His screams brought her back. When she was unable to utter those words, he tortured her with the snake, allowing it to crawl over her nude body—its memory to be etched within her eternal mind. The scales projected the same filthy sensation she had when he touched her skin. The only way she could ever be clean again would be to have all her skin pulled off.

His intense gaze indicated a change in his demeanor. It was then that he raped her with the snake, telling her how he was going to let it crawl up inside of her; how it would gnaw at her organs until they were completely destroyed; how it would lay eggs inside of her that would hatch and then crawl around until they, too, found their way out; how they would gnaw and bite to make a hole for escape; how it would stay inside of her, crawling through her stomach and up her throat until it found its way out of her body through her mouth; how it would venture out and retreat because people around her would be trying to kill it. As he was shoving the snake inside of her, she closed her eyes.

When she was conscious again, the snake and the canvas bag were gone. The beast was raping her and whispering nasty sexual comments. The hate she experienced was building unconquerable mountains, screaming to be released from a shattered mind.

I waited high upon the shelf knowing once he was gone, the other me's would have to join together to salvage what was left.

CHAPTER 10

The trestle stood tall and straight, adorning the river filled with the season's rains. Its image made my knees weak, my head light. It was such a high structure standing alone against nature's canvas. Much higher than the trees, I surmised it to be the tallest train crossing around. I'm not sure it was still in use—it had such a lonely look. I thought of the commonalities it shared with me. Loneliness, abandonment, silence—the trestle and me. It always captured my attention. I was drawn to it. There was a power about it that disallowed resistance, monopolizing every spark of the mind demandingly calling my name. Passing and not looking was impossible. It focused in on my attention as long as it was visible. I had acknowledged the silent issue with both the trestle and my father. Silence—the most controlling variable I would ever encounter.

The silence was particularly controlling now that he had forced his silence upon me. Every thought in my head could be controlled by him. Looking at the trestle was captivating as it called out. My father had experienced it, too, stopping the car to gaze. I felt his eyes plastered to my body. I closed my eyes, keeping my back to him. I did not want to look at him or the trestle. His way of reading my mind was disturbing. I could never understand how he knew my thoughts. Did I reveal them to him?

My "why" search had started once again. My thinking! I could not stay alert, my thinking following tangents. How high the trestle looked! I wondered how deep the river ran. It was difficult for me to image a jump—or fall—from the top. Would the water be cold and snaky?

Feeling a hand on my leg, my father said calmly, "There's a lot of space between the trestle and the water. People call this Snake River because of all the snakes. They nest around the supports in the water. That way, when something falls from the trestle, they can attack...."

His voice continued, becoming faint as my mind focused on his statements. Scared of both heights and snakes, I made avoiding both of these a priority. His words focused my attention. If he had said anything important, I had missed it. But then, he would repeat it sometime in the near future. It was not so important *what* he said, but rather, *how* he said it. I would hear it again when he decided that application of his message was appropriate and urgent. I always had to stay on guard. Otherwise, I wouldn't be prepared. It wasn't the actual rape I had to prepare for, but rather, the thinking. I needed that to survive.

Driving home, my thoughts pondered the trestle. It held such horrible and devastating potential. Once again, the time piece was the focus. Arriving home, he laughed as he walked ahead of me. It was nice to have him a distance from me. Being behind him was more safe than being ahead. This way I could observe his behavior. Somehow, the anticipation of the terror was easier to take when he was always in my visual field. Not necessarily easier, but more manageable. It was the distance that provided time for me to perceive the danger.

My immediate goal was to make it to my room—alone! That would be the only solution to my problems—withdrawal. It sounded so nice! But, he always invaded my alone times, preventing the actualization of my plans.

Ascending the stairs, I scurried into my room. Alone! I tried mentally to list possible times I could be alone. Unless he died, my aloneness would not be possible. Death—it would be so acceptable. I concentrated on that, acknowledging it would take a lot of determination to murder. I had never planned to kill anything. I had always been such a good girl. Why was I planning to do this? Once I had killed him, would I continue and kill more? Perhaps my mother? She had abandoned me and allowed the abuse. Mentally, I tried to visualize what the room would look like; what expression he would have on his face; what his blood would smell like; whether he would laugh as he died; could I torture him as he had me; would he beg as I had so many times; or would I allow him to beg? My mind had been my only friend for such a long time, why was it now becoming evil? Why was I becoming evil? Had the abuse taken away more of me than I realized? There were no answers!

Always on the run, I felt compelled to avoid him forever. It was impossible, despite the compelling drive. Being torn between this force and the reality of its failure compounded the already present problems. Murder appeared to be one of two answers. Murder or suicide? Either would resolve the issue. Careful planning was required of either. The real dilemma being which deserved to live and which deserved to die. Only I knew the option I would choose.

His presence in my room was sudden, one of importance. Looking at him produced those horrible moments of disgust spent with him. A forever dirtiness—the status of my life. What did he want? What did he always want? Sex! He never spent any time with me anymore that he wasn't concentrating on sex or terror. I had learned well. His sexual training was ingrained forever within my memory.

Sitting on my bed, he began his mental search of my body; his facial expressions changing. His definitive destructive character found delight in his search. Moving his hands toward me made me uncomfortable. I left him there with one of the other me's below my shelf of safety as I watched with disgust our rapist. His eyes plastered onto her as his hands became roaming torpedoes, aggressive and uncaring. The intense, painful squeezing of her breasts was unbearable. His resentful kissing accompanied his stripping of her body. Undressing himself, he was eager to proceed as he pushed her back onto the bed; his mouth roaming about her breasts as he entered his penis. His release was rapid and unnerving. Rolling away, he demanded oral sex.

This was so repulsive a thought to all of us that it produced nausea. It had to be done if she wanted him out of here. Beginning to follow his commands, she felt the warning from her queasy stomach. The worst possible action this precise moment would be the unsettling of her stomach. Her muscles contracted! And immediately, the vomiting began. Horror erupted! Throwing her off the bed; he angrily went to the shower. She was free for the moment, but he would be back.

His return with the same angry expression was enough to evoke an immediate apology. He walked across the room, grabbed a handful of hair and shouted, "Get your ass in the car!"

She did as ordered. Her mind reflected the images of pain and lust, knowing that within the next few hours she would experience both. The silent wait with inward torment was commencing once again.

The drive was in the direction of the trestle. My fears immediately bombarded me. I had experienced and survived various torments. I tried to decide which one it would be tonight. Any one of them brought about those horrid feelings I had reexperienced earlier in the day. Maybe the trestle was calling my name now to end all the abuse. There may be a little hope after all. I had already convinced myself that God takes the spirit of a person before the body dies, so you never experience the actual impact of death. What my philosophy was based on, I do not know, but it was a comforting theory.

As the car stopped, I recognized the surroundings. We were at the trestle. I cringed as he ordered me out of the car.

Shocked, I pleaded, "Please don't make me go out there!"

Coldly, he said, "This is what happens when you don't obey."

Taking my hand, we walked out onto the trestle. Looking down in the dark was more frightening than looking at it from the road. There was no way of telling how high it really was. I could hear the water hitting against the supports. It sounded far away, or maybe the water was just turbulent. It wasn't important. I just needed to stay on top of the trestle. Everything else was trivial.

I summoned all the other me's as I sensed the terror tonight would be more than any, or all of us, would be able to survive. Climbing upon the shelf, I watched the alignment of the many me's. Perhaps it was the coolness of the air or the height of the trestle or just all the fear that created a me just for this—a terror too great for my memory.

He sat down on the trestle, moving a lantern to his side. He unzipped his trousers. Lowering them to his knees and sitting down, he motioned her over. She moved. Once beside him, he demanded oral sex. His implicit order was for her to keep her mouth on his penis until told to remove it. This thought was repulsive, but the thought of being dropped from the trestle was also. It was a choice between two evils. She had to discern which was the lesser evil—the one she could survive.

Death is a scary concept. And the necessary element for it was missing. She didn't have the stomach for his demands. Out of fear of death, she fulfilled his demands. Gagging, she tried to keep the contents of her stomach settled. To vomit on him again tonight would mean too much torture. Swallowing the vomit, she continued until he withdrew his penis.

His next order was to clean his penis with her tongue. She followed this order, thinking the nightmare would end soon. When directed by him, she stopped. He stood up ordering her to join him, reiterating that any command he gave was to be followed quickly or she would regret the noncompliance.

She felt sick and dizzy. Her knees hurt. Her ears listened for the water. Any moment he could toss her over, bringing unequivocal terror. He had lost her trust a long time ago. She was so frightened of him that she really thought he would kill her, if not intentionally, accidentally.

Watching him, we all waited for his next move. Her stomach was becoming more and more queasy. We knew she was going to be sick. Trying to swallow the contents of her stomach each time it returned to her mouth was too much. It just could not stay down. Without warning, the repeated vomiting commenced. She had accidentally vomited on her rapist for the second time in the same evening.

Fear seized her body, awaiting the thrust of his anger. Suddenly, a large beast lunged toward her. We all started to scream! Nothing came out. His arm went around her, sweeping her body up and into the air. Stepping up closer to the edge of the trestle, she began begging him not to throw her over. For the first time in a very long time, we wanted his skin touching us. She held on with all her strength. His demands to remove her hold on him were not heeded. She intended to hold on to him even if it meant his going over with her. Dropping his arms from under her legs, he pried her arms from his neck. The water was her destination. Screaming obscenities, he pushed her over the edge.

Falling, she screamed. It seemed to take a long time to

hit the water, which pushed up the ribs into her lungs, piercing the eyes, leaving visions of the much-dreaded snakes. The entrance seemed never to end, almost as if the river was pulling her down into a bottomless pit. Her chest felt tight, too tight to endure. There was a light-headedness as the water swallowed her up into its swell. It would soon be over—all the abuse, all the horror, all the pain. The downward motion changed. She was moving upward. With thoughts of drowning, she broke the surface. Gasping, her lungs sucked in huge gulps of air. It felt good.

Above her, she heard his wicked laugh. She was in the water and would have to swim to get out. She was a good swimmer. But could she outswim the snakes? Or would they coil around her body, biting, killing? Overwhelmed, she swam, praying the snakes would stay away. The longer she swam, the more fear was sensed. There was a part of her that rationalized the possibility he had lied about the snakes. He had lied many times without regard to her safety. Maybe she wasn't swimming with snakes after all. She was getting tired, but the fear of even one snake in the river propelled her forward. The images of snakes getting entangled in her long hair was unthinkable. Regardless of how tired she became, she had to keep swimming.

After a very long, long swim, she began to touch bottom. The legs were so tired, she wanted to stop, to float and to let the body rest for just a few minutes. Visions of snakes would not allow it. Continuing, she felt her knees touch bottom. Exhausted, she came to rest in the mud. The legs refused to cooperate as she stood up. A little more rest was needed if she was to continue.

She had to find where she had swum to and how she could get home. Walking entered her mind. Staying there until dawn entered her mind but was rejected for fear of the snakes. She ran her fingers through her hair, making sure no snakes were entwined. His push over the trestle had not killed her, nor had she encountered any snakes. This me had survived his hellish torture; and once again, all the me's merged together to mend the horrors of the night.

Sitting in the muddy river, I made the decision to walk home. The darkness prevented a clear synthesis of the terrain, but there did appear to be a slight hill I would have to climb. The only light I remembered was a street light where we entered. If I had judged appropriately, I should be able to get out somewhere in that vicinity. The walk home would be lengthy. Thoughts of harm coming to me were upsetting. The idea of being raped along the roadside was overwhelming, not because of the nature of the crime or my age, but due to my father continually raping me; I could not endure even one more rape by anyone. My thoughts precluded my aloneness by the river. Walking slowly and carefully, I spotted the lone light. I would find my way to it.

His laughter was drifting into my ears as my rapist was waiting for my arrival. It was so odd how he could read my thoughts, absorbing my strategies without any communication. Defeatedly, I walked toward the laughter. There was no need to debate the issue of getting home. He had, once again, outsmarted me. My mind and body were too tired to process any more tonight. So, with great desolation, I sat down in the car to ride home in silence. There was no hope in me. The dark cloud floating above my head had rained upon me once again.

I showered, cleaning the filth from my body, but not from my mind. I didn't know if I could. I just wanted to go to bed. Pulling the covers over my head, I curled up in my bed. I was safe there—the world was pushed away. The covers prevented its return. This was the darkness that felt safe. This was my refuge. The longer I was there, the more safe I felt. I wanted to stay there forever. There was no reason why I would want to venture out. It was just me here keeping me safe. I was once again in my world where beasts, snakes, and trestles were unknown.

CHAPTER 11

The others had multiplied and received their respective dress symbolic of the event and emotion. The number seemed to grow and grow, each remaining just as vivid as the day of their creation. They all had great importance to her for comfort, survival, an expression of horror in one's life. Perhaps it was the summer which made the splitting different this time. There had been few conflicts within the many me's until that summer's heavy terror began.

Spring was not a season I warmly anticipated, despite all its wondrous events unfolding a bright fresh make-over of winter's dreadful toll. It is a season of vivid memories. A season of pain, humiliation, terror. The kind of terror resultant of strange men having access to your body with unlimited liberties.

I listened intently when my father's mood altered. That total change in affect prior to abusive behaviors was etched within my memory. With a heightened difference tonight, his pacings up and down the hallway increased my level of consciousness. Something was amiss. I dreaded becoming its target.

Abruptly, he passed through my doorway with that cold, distant stare that sank my spirits. The dread of becoming its target ended. Avoiding his glance, I prayed for an escape. The touch of his hand upon my arm evoked anxiety, turmoil, nausea. My racing thought compelled my driven desire for escape. Ignoring his touch wasn't an option, and responding to his touch was too repulsive.

Suspended in time, waiting for the world to continue its motion, seconds seemed like hours. Although terrorized, I was still safe. That was, as long as time remained suspended. The abuse would start soon—all too soon. Fear consumed my storming thoughts, visualizing the recurrence of his intrusive violations. Time was the controlling force—the reassuring force, my thinking. Often the thoughts of his cruelty overpowered my mind, holding it prisoner until the abuse commenced. Then, I merely had to hold onto what reality should be rather than was. And, if I was lucky, I would lose consciousness, becoming oblivious to his terror.

The quietness of the drive to the lakehouse cued me as to the awaiting terror. I hated this drive—a drive that just years earlier had been of impatience, yearning to be where the rest of the world seemed to fade away. My special place where the attention and adoration of my father was captured. My heart yearned for those times and for the dad I knew then. What had I done? Was this the way it would be forever? Could it get any worse? There never seemed to be a way out. When would my father just die, leaving my soul in rest? Why did I have to live in this? And where had fairness been lost? There never seemed to be any answers; but then, the abuse always began again before I could learn the answers.

Perhaps it was his shouting which interfered with my "why" search. Or his big hand pulling me from the car. That was it tonight. My thoughts halted as he pulled on me. I think, perhaps, I missed his order, being absorbed in my "why" search. Falling at his feet jolted me to the present. Thinking was no longer critical. Survival had become the issue.

Numbness creases the soul when hell lurks to circumvent its destiny. An eternal haunting as one mortal destroys another. An existence, but yet, a nonexistence. As I stumbled, he pushed me through the door. Larger than normal liquor and food supplies were stacked on the floor. I sensed only a small miracle could intervene and prevent his anticipated pleasures. Waiting for the impact in silent desperation, I realized there would be no one to come to my aid.

Watching the arrival of the other men frightened me. They were strangers. Why were they here, where these visits had become weekends of lustful abuse? I shrieked at the thought of these men watching the usual rituals. Never did I think they would become actual participants. Somehow these thoughts were not inclusive of my cognitive processes; nor should they have been for a fifteen-year-old girl.

I tried to think what other girls my age were doing and with whom. My stomach twisted as the memories attacked. My skin yearning to crawl off my bones, searching for a shelter from his exposed filth. There was no escape. Closed in on all sides, being stalked by the oncoming slaughter of my body and emotions, I could only wait. There was nothing else to do. Time again was the controlling force in my life. The added variable—alcohol and perverted imaginations of sexual lust. The cruelty of time enhanced my fears, bringing the terror more into focus.

I found my way into the room cluttered with memories too bizarre and hurtful to recall. There was no haven here, at least not accessible to me. Laughter and voices trailed down the hallway, imposing upon my hearing while chills fleshed my skin. Oh, if I could just die! I wouldn't have to think about this anymore. It would all be over. Smells deterred my thoughts. Smoked salmon and cigarettes stifled the air. Alcohol talk would soon join, coupled with the smells and touches of lust.

A drink in hand, he boldly trodded into my world. His familiar distant stare remained focused as my heart pounded loudly, swiftly drowning out all other sounds. Breathing deeply, he tossed a package onto the bed. Obedient to his harsh order, I removed the article from the box. Gasping, I stared at the sheer flesh-tone robe, very short, very accessible. Horrified, I realized the evening's intent.

Stillness paralyzed my being. That helpless moment when any action is detrimental to the soul. Scared, I did nothing. His grinding teeth captured my attention. Hurriedly, he pulled at my clothing. Terrified, I moved away, placing distance between his rage and myself. Failing, I awaited the deliverance of his aggression. Standing above me, he smiled as he stripped my body. Without speaking, he slipped the transparent robe around my nude body. My heart sank. My fears became reality. I wanted so much to just die before any further actualizations. Instead, I floated to the invisible shelf far from their reaches.

Sitting quietly upon it, I watched the desecration of her soul begin to unfold. Her rapist taking more and more of an already depleted soul, laughingly shouting his demands to join his guests. Escorting her through the door, the moment of dread arrived. Every eye turned their way. Hands reached out . . . mouths whistled. She wanted to cry, to believe she would awaken soon, and the last few years of her life would be different. She had to escape—somehow.

No escape! The room was sealed. She was outnumbered. Trembling and resisting as a sleazy man pulled her onto his lap, she moved away, backing into another. Casting her eyes about the room, she received that familiar and controlling look from her father, creating total passivity. The pawing of hands heightened her fearful apprehensions. Her eyes looked to the floor, to the ceiling—anywhere, but in their faces. Their fun was at her expense. Their jeering statements filled her head; their beckonings made her dizzy. What was her father doing? And why? How could he let these men do this? How could he sit there watching all of this?

"Please make them stop!" she screamed. Everything stopped. There was a glimmer of internal hope her nightmare would end. The stillness of the room was frightening. No one moved, no one spoke. The other me fled her captors to merge once again.

Safety, how unsure it is when at the mercy of others; how short its change to destruction; and how heavy the burden prior to change, like weights tied to weakened ankles. The torment of the body's yearning for safety ignites those tiny wrinkles of time altered by the desires of others. The crashing of the ego when one discovers the safety net broken. The desolation of hope. The death of the spirit.

Hours had passed. I wanted to rest, finding that trance state between awakefulness and sleep, where my full attention could be exerted, preserving my sanity. The preservation of sanity, those obsessive-compulsive behaviors whose purpose is useless. The counting, the listing, the cleaning, the naming of everything. They function to restore the sanity so ravishly depleted. They were my comfort, my stability. Frequently providing a ritual to diminish the anticipated pain. Always to seal the lust cognitively making life appear manageable. They were the bridges I crossed each time when returning from the abuse. Sometimes a long bridge, sometimes a short bridge. But, always a bridge never to be burned. One to be cherished as the only access for return.

Evening ages slowly when one is watching time. And with that process, one measures the possibilities and the impossibilities. Above all, one measures the probability, that is, just how strong the odds are that once alcohol had inhibited their emotions, I would again have the terror of these men. Their noise penetrated my silent room like sparks in smoldering ashes. The power they had far surpassed the one possibility I had of escape. Their laughter and joking reminded me just how small my chance was.

Without warning, the door opened. My heart fell to the floor! My stomach muscles wrenched with panic! Hoping against hope, I recognized the birth of failure. My father had come for me. The expected rituals were commencing. His distant glazed stare was becoming highly controlling. So controlling, I knew it was useless to resist, which would mean physical aggression with his fists on my face. Not fighting him sexually prevented the physical abuse. Grabbing my arm, he led me to his guests. Strange what the mind thinks when facing adversity, danger, exploitation. Believing I could avoid the pain by not making eye contact; believing my father wasn't going to follow through with all of this; and believing that this horrible nightmare would end soon. My beliefs were weak. My desperation was strong.

The loneliness of violence creates moments of silence as preparation of the descent emerges. Not knowing which would initiate the onslaught, I stood in fear. Pleading didn't work. Resistance would only ensure more abuse. Compliance, willfully, was despicable. I had to think. Thinking would get me through whatever was to happen. I would be okay. This day, too, would soon pass. It always did. I would find a haven somewhere, somehow. Whatever had been planned would not change.

I tried to prepare myself for the worst imaginable acts, but found my mind focused on the shelf with all its safety. Her mind screamed relentlessly. The terror intended by the group was overwhelming. It was unreal! Soon she would awaken to find this nightmare to be finished—gone!

Releasing a slight chuckle, he led her to a bed in full view of all those present. She hesitated. Quickly, he ordered her to obey. Without the courage to resist, she complied. As he pulled the robe from her, she wanted to be hidden from the view of these other men. She wanted her nude body shielded. Embarrassed and afraid, she was forcibly raped by her father in the presence of his guests. They watched as he took liberty after liberty. Their lustful stares invaded her thoughts. Their moans and groans at anticipation grew louder and louder as he continued. They were delighted to see this man rape his own daughter. They were eagerly awaiting their turn.

Men are indeed exquisite creatures. Intellectualizing any issue on command, yet becoming a mindless beast waiting impatiently for quick gratification at the expense of others. That's where hatred comes from, and how it silently and hastily grows into a malignancy thriving from its unknown nesting ground, where the limited expression of hate births the internal growth and design for future vindication. That kind of grudge where destruction is livid within the soul controlled by expected mores. Pain so well contained that only death would be a viable solution. She wanted to kill him! She wanted to kill them all for watching him do this and not helping.

The time element was different tonight. It wasn't the long drawn out ritual with anal and oral sex. He appeared to be setting a precedent, or perhaps he was tired. Once his passion was released, he signaled to the others.

One by one, each stepped forward to participate in her rape. Each with a look of contentment. Each with a look of evil. One by one, they raped her. Everyone watched as each violation took place, some laughing, some moaning, as if experiencing and reexperiencing that moment. Her mind wanted to say it was all over. Everyone had had a turn. Somehow she knew it was just beginning.

The silence of the room was uncomfortable. Laughing, her father pushed her down onto the soiled odoriferous linens of lust, repeating his rape. Suddenly, he appeared oblivious to the presence of others. Using cords, he tied her hands and feet, establishing her position to be for some time, making her more conscious of the men with their stares. There was nothing to hide behind or beneath. She was in clear view of everyone. And again, each took his turn with anal and oral sex being the focus. She recognized the numbness spreading throughout her body, wanting it to reach her mind. Abruptly, all the men finished with their fantasies. There was a chance of release.

She wanted to shield herself from their view and their filth. She commenced thinking, only to find her mind questioning why no one objected to the "fun" they were having, why no one questioned her age, and why no one perceived these events as unusual. Perhaps they were as disturbed as her father. Perhaps these events were more common than she thought. There were even times she thought her father was right, and this was the way sex was taught. Retrospectively, it was these times when she was dangerously close to being suctioned into the vile and wicked world which surrounded her. There were many questions, but no answers. And that poor girl was virtually ripped apart by her father and his guests. The poundings upon her, the laughs, the nasty talk, the constant line of rapist after rapist until the early hours of the morning, all working to destroy this other me.

Hours passed. Pulling at the cords, she anticipated more abuse. When she could not loosen them, she sensed a need for preparation. She wanted to convince herself that being nude in front of them was not that noticeable anymore. They had seen her nude body. Perhaps they wouldn't look. Perhaps they would depart soon. But time passed—they stayed. She watched closely as her father began his pacings. Shortly, he departed.

Upon his return, he had brought with him two cameras. These were not the kind of memories to photograph. Oh, how she wanted to run away! Screaming and laughing, he photographed her nude body along with the other men. He appeared to be quite proud of his action, smiling as he encouraged the men to ravish. The movie camera was started. She hated him! Smilingly, he laid his body by hers, lustfully pawing and pawing as he destroyed his own flesh and blood. How she wished she could penetrate his chest, yanking his heart out and slamming it onto the floor to burst into fragments as his vile, wicked self had done to this child.

His slight chuckling was audible amidst the other voices cheering him on until he indicated for them to join her on the bed. Three alcohol tainted men began their pawing and raping. While one raped her, one was fondling her breasts. The remaining one was shoving his penis into her mouth. No one did anything to stop this madness. Her efforts to resist brought a fist slamming into her face. She tried to think of things to absorb her pain, to think of ways to get revenge for all these violations, but she couldn't think of anything to suffice. Her mind was sluggish.

"Tell me what you want!" her father demanded. "Tell me how many of these men you can take on tonight. Are you enough woman to take us all on?"

There was no comment. Angered, he grabbed her neck squeezing until she could barely breathe. Then, he stopped.

Close to her face, he said, "What do I have to do to make you tell me what you want?"

"I want to be left alone!" she pleaded, looking into his face.

She immediately knew she had erred into more suffering. She held her breath as he walked outside. No one in the room left. A man began stroking his hand on her breasts. Just as he moved his mouth down to her breasts, her father returned, carrying a canvas bag. He stepped away.

The same identical demands were voiced again, choking

her mind at the thought of saying those horrible and nasty words. She remained silent.

Turning around, he reached into the canvas bag pulling out a snake as he said, "Tell me what you want or I'm going to let this snake crawl up you."

Signaling to the men, he summoned two over to the bed.

Laughing, he said, "Tell this man you want him to fuck you, or I'll send this snake up you." She hesitated in horror.

Taking the snake, he pushed the snake inside of her. Screaming, she complied with his wishes. The night continued in that fashion until everyone's tired thirst for sex was squelched. As everyone was falling asleep or leaving, the cords were cut. She found a haven in the shower, but the filth was embedded and was to remain a part of her forever.

This was wrong to do to anyone, especially your own child. The frustration—the filth, the continuous knowledge of never being clean. The variances in the wants, the voices, the lips, the bodies—too close, too loud, too sweaty, too wet. Horror! She had to forget. By whatever measures it called for, she would have to make all of this go away. She would convince herself all this madness was only within her mind. Transgressions of the mind to be experienced, but not acknowledged as having ever occurred.

Parents aren't suppose to let this happen. Why were these different? Her mind was racing—too many thoughts in too little time. There needed to be more of the me's to deal with all these thoughts. Thoughts which often contradicted those of the previous me's over and over. Thoughts so opposite, some supporting, some defeating, so conflicted and appalling, they seem to long for separate entities. And the me sitting safely upon the invisible shelf simply divided the personality into two. Twins, identical in all respects with the exception of thought patterns. One overshadowed with darkness and one adorned with hope. Destructive and nurturing, the two never merged, as one always remained separate to deal with the emotions of lust.

Morning broke with the leftover memories of the night. The smells of lust forever jammed into my nostrils. My partially working legs and stomach were sore from the night. My chest was pressed inward with pain, but most of all, my mind hurt. There was no logic in these happenings. I didn't know these men, but what would I do if I saw them again? What would I say? What might they say? How could my father do this?

His entrance into the room broke my concentrated thoughts. Standing in front of me, nude, he chuckled before getting onto the bed. His mouth rested on my breasts, biting as his hands hastily removed my clothes. My sore body was casting doubt if it could function until he was finished. The roughness of his manner increased my pain. My body had been abused; there were no parts without that throbbing pain. His saliva being left behind nauseated me as I groped for the invisible shelf.

Gritting her teeth, she hoped for endurance. His penis entered her, his mouth on her breasts, his hands grabbed her buttocks. The highly aggressive back and forth movements were accompanied by his verbal demands for the body he ravished to respond. How she hated all of this! Soon he would be finished, and then, perhaps, she could be alone. It seemed as though she lived in two worlds, the world with the abuse and the dream of being the only living soul on a deserted island.

I found refuge in the shower, trying to wash his scum away. I needed to turn myself inside out to scrub the filth out of my body. I scrubbed and scrubbed until my skin was raw and still felt so very, very dirty. I felt such monumental shame in what they had done. I didn't think I would survive, nor was that my wish. I hated this secret, and I hated him for bringing these men. I hated everything about life. I hated my parents, but most of all, I hated me. Why did this happen? Lost in my "why" search, I was unaware when he walked into the room. Holding the photographs in one hand and the movie reel in the other, he threatened to distribute them openly if I told of the weekend's escapades. Terrorized and embarrassed, I agreed to keep quiet. Suddenly, I needed the invisible shelf for comfort, for reassurance that silence was the better of my options. Perhaps I was calling a conference of the different me's in hopes of resolving the dilemma.

It had been different this time. He made her hate herself intensely, to think of death, to yearn for death, to self-abuse until all life is removed. Then the me's struggled to survive, to fight to remain in this war of life that was always a defeat. And, many times a defeat asked to be handed down. A war bringing devastation with each, leaving an adamant demand for survival.

The two opposing forces forever in conflict, with one fueling the devastation of the other. Senselessness enmeshed their worlds, disallowing logic, acceptance, complacency. The result—eternal bitterness and frustration trapped within the power of yet another opposing and deadly beast whose perception of death was slow and torturous, tedious and humiliating. No resolution, no consolation, just a vicious cycle of hurt after hurt. One of the me's always in search of the tragic error she made, inflicting herself with a life of hell; always in search of death; always losing the grip of death, just to become the target of his brutal violations once again. Such a wasted life, breathing air that could be used by one more worthy. Oh, how her breath being exhaled must have killed the surrounding life. Pity this lonely creature seemed to invariably escape her intense yearning for death, only enjoying its taste.

This shattered life with all the other me's had seemed so

simple before now, with the total conflict being external versus its present internal status. It was easy to know the source of the conflict. All the horrid frustration of having it with her and never being free. Funny, how no one acknowledges enslavement of the soul until the desolation of being another's ploy drags on and on through years of entanglement in the sick, sick mind of others. It brings about irreparable shatterings deep, deep inside, birthing that compelling urge to look back at every shattering, full of fear as each violation is relived time and time again.

Hatred filled crevices within her mind, glossed with repugnancy, desperately screaming, "Die! Die! Die!" Her steps becoming conflicted by her twin lovingly nurturing the wounded other, repeatedly assuring her she shared no blame for his actions, that it would end soon, that the body heals in time and the mind somehow survives, that the day would come when he could no longer transgress his passions upon her, that she could be her guardian angel attending the cuts, the scrapes, and the battered mind, gently pillowing her head as the violations ceased.

Quite often she spoke of the innocence of the me's, the unnaturalness of his acts, the expected response sexually from one organ stimulating the other regardless of its source. It was always those words that shut her away from the other me's. The pleasantness of what she felt just that one time made everything much worse. It was wrong! It was horrifying! Nothing quieted the internal storm of this me. At least, it had not happened with him, but rather one of his guests. That way it cast a faint shadow of acceptance. Many times she told herself of the normalcy of her response. It happens to everyone at one point or another. Why was there pleasure in something so filthy? Why did all of this happen? Please, please won't someone take all of this away? Bury these different me's? Stop! She had to stop.

This mental rampage only created more me's as its pain worked its path from the right side of her head around to the left, increasing in intensity until, at last, the pain would subside, quieting the other me's, thus temporarily ending the conflicted twins. Their purpose and their conflicts shelved at least for the moment, not on the invisible shelf, but rather, on a mental shelf inside her head.

The interchanging of the me's had begun to feel rather comfortable, especially for the twins providing a sense of stability, perhaps the only stability anywhere. The number of the me's and the intensity of them were of no concern. Rather, the expected arrival of the new ones. There was a need to eliminate conflicts, to simplify the situational factors, to mold and temper the already present me's with the emotions of the new, to create the exact number of me's necessary to live in her private world.

And what about living a life? Wasn't that what all the others were about? Struggling to survive or too cowardly to die, they had, thus far, created a balance between those wishing death and those wishing life. More and more me's were to follow, but for now, all time was consumed with the ones present. The more emphatic me was the one thinking of the irony should she learn to enjoy these times, to willingly participate, perhaps even initiate the lustful acts he had taught so well. Would it bring closure to a nightmare many years old? Would it intensify the madness? Would it make all things go away? Would it give her a life without further violations? The chances for her happiness seemed less and less. Her darkest thoughts always eluded any glimmer of happiness. The shelf held fast as the darkness of life progressed, and when the violations had ceased, she dressed the other me's, covering the filth, forging within her personality all the horrors of the years passed.

CHAPTER 12

I cannot discern if I was frightened or humiliated into silence that spring weekend. Whatever its origin, the silence came with an obsession to die. The enduring of many things from my father and the inclusion of his guests pushed my determination. Suicide is a difficult issue, particularly for one so young, and I was well aware I did not have the necessary element to take my own life. Violence—a part of my life far too long—was not acceptable. But I could accept a passive suicide. And suicide, regardless of its method, still has the same result. I was ready to make my preparations.

Actually, my father provided the method for my plan. Weight was one of his major issues. Strangely, only a few pounds added could disturb his entire mode, evoking intense opposition. He had, unknowingly, established my route of freedom from his abuse. He had formulated my death. I now had a second secret about my father—one he knew, and one he did not.

Discretion was the optimum element in my plan. Without it, the plan would be foiled. I couldn't risk it. Eating would stay a part of my routine. Added would be induced vomiting. A simple plan that should go completely unnoticed. Initially, everything ran smoothly. Having failed to think of the weekend rituals, and that getting a few minutes to purge would be impossible, frustrated me. With summer approaching, there would be more days spent at the lakehouse, giving me less time to purge. Modifications were mandated if I was to succeed. Exercise was added and then increased. Sleep was discontinued for most nights. That time was for running, wearing several pairs of socks to soften my footsteps. The sound of my feet hitting seemed too loud. I added more socks. Then, I could run without being heard. No one would know.

Eating, purging, running. Eating, purging, running. The cycle continued. Dedicated to making my plan work, I watched for opportunities when a meal could be skipped without being noticed. For every meal omitted, I could exercise longer, losing more weight. Substituting low calorie foods for high calorie foods would help facilitate the plan. It would appear that I was eating continuously but would really be taking in fewer calories. It was the calories that bothered me. I was so defenseless against them. They reminded me of my rapist. Their silent attack as they sneak upon people.

I became obsessed with the calorie battle. Counting and calculating, the goal was to omit more calories, yet give the appearance that I was eating. After careful planning, I was able to elaborate my plan. I would be seen holding food, biting food, and chewing food, but there would be no swallowing. If I could do this throughout the day, then I could relax at meal times, when he would be watching. I would have a good reason for not eating. And my only hunger was that of freedom. It was so close, I could almost touch it. Mentally, I savored all freedom had to give, knowing that soon my body would be free.

Changes were taking place. Pounds were disappearing. Bones were protruding, clearly identifying their location under my skin. I knew my plan was working! I continued my regimen with true contentment and realization I would soon be free of the abuse that had driven me to death. The savoring of that freedom fueled my desire. Somehow there wasn't a fear of death this time. It felt quite comfortable, almost reassuring. The approaching escape made any abuse I endured until then manageable. That was my thought during my nightly runs.

It was almost over. I was almost free of all the terror and all the abuse. There would be no more rapes by him nor his guests. There would be no more objects, no more snakes, no more trestles, no more coffins, no more guests, no more anything. I wouldn't hurt anymore. I wouldn't feel dirty anymore. I would, at last, be free. Freedom and happiness of that freedom was the thought trudging across my mind, when suddenly someone stepped out into my path. My heart pounded. I couldn't breathe. I didn't have a strategy. This was not suppose to happen! Mortified, I stood in shock. Time seemed to hold still. I couldn't think. The figure in front of me gave a slight chuckle. The sound was all too familiar—it was my rapist. Unsure of what he might do, I did nothing. It seemed like hours we just stood staring. Two mortals frozen in time and place. I knew I would not be the first to move. He would break the trance when he was ready.

Silence! How uncomfortable silence was when shared with him. The threat of his image. He enjoyed the moments of silence, moments of torture for me. That's why he did it. He enjoyed torturing me. With his familiar laugh, he took my hand and walked toward the house. No explanation was needed. He never asked what I was doing or why. He was going to rape me. I would be okay. This, too, would pass. It always did. That's why he continued. There was no one to stop him. I tried to wish him away. And when I failed, I wished myself upon the shelf.

He began his ritual. The kissing, the fondling, and then the demands for sexual statements. He was almost gentle, becoming more aggressive and hostile when she failed to converse in his language. Squeezing his hands around her throat, he convinced her to utter the words that gave him such great pleasure. Pushing her onto the floor, his mouth moved from her mouth onto her chest. Pulling at her clothes, he proceeded to satisfy his lustful pleasures. Painfully and slowly, he became a savage beast as he bit, pulled, and squeezed. As the minutes passed, she concentrated on her freedom so close at hand. Nothing was going to stand in the way. She could endure the moment because it was one of the few remaining.

Satisfied, he sat on the floor touching her stomach. Moving his hand along her body, he commented how pronounced her bone structure was becoming. Cringing at the fear he may interrupt her suicide plan, she agreed to eat more. He was content. Watching her dress, he appeared to be questioning something. He was too close for comfort. She wanted him away before he recognized her plan.

He walked away, leaving her alone. The other me's quietly and sobbingly nurtured her back to some level, but there seemed to be parts which were missing, or perhaps too many parts were present. I felt my skin crawling with filth. I had to wash his scent, his thoughts, his touches off my body. I needed a barrier between his memories and me. The shower—the water—the barrier! I could, for the moment, forget his lust. Vomiting would discard his saliva left in my mouth from his repulsive kisses. I would feel better—soon. I vomited and scrubbed, vomited and scrubbed, until my stomach was empty and my raw skin burning. Breakfast would be soon. I anticipated a heavy meal with much insistence of large portions. I would comply, but I would also purge until I was sure none of it remained in me.

Walking down to breakfast, I felt dizzy and unsteady. I had to make it through breakfast with no obstacles. My plan was right on target. It was somewhat more difficult, but it was working. I continued my regimen for several more weeks. It was then that my problem developed. More and more abuse had driven me to induce more vomiting and increase exercises. I had lost more weight. It was now a problem. I had no energy and couldn't support my weight for any length of time. I was scared, but reassured that my freedom was close.

Overconfidence is a quality I never had until that moment. Somewhere along the way, I had acquired an overconfident approach to my suicide plan. It was infallible. I was already enjoying what I thought would be benefits. Nothing could invalidate my strategy. It was such a relief to have the end so near. I was absorbing the glimpse of freedom while walking through the house. There were good memories there, too. There just weren't enough of them to equate with the bad. I bid farewell to those happy times with sadness. I bid farewell to the bad times with much relief. The time had come. That was my last thought.

Opening my eyes, I glanced around the room. I was hospitalized. My plan had failed. I was crushed. Someone had taken my chance for freedom away, and I was once again a prisoner of my father. There was no end to my nightmare, only more terror. I was determined to complete my plan. I wanted to die and had almost done it. I would not quit! The IV in place was quickly yanked out. I was going to win the first battle of my life. Lack of knowledge and unclear thinking supported my determination. I did not know my plan would be interrupted by forced feeding.

Weeks passed and life looked much better. There was no sexual abuse while hospitalized. I was safe from him as long as I remained where I was. I don't know what my father did for his pleasures. It became apparent that waiting was not his forte. Threats of distributing the photos and tape of the past spring were voiced. Unless my weight increased and I was discharged, everyone would have accessibility to the pornographic material. My father knew precisely what to use to intimidate me. I would do anything to escape the humiliation he threatened.

I continued to gain weight during the next week, until my father's visit one day created my death wish once again. There had been a decrease in the staff's constant supervision, allowing me more private time. The bathroom was no longer locked to prevent my purging. The wastebasket was no longer checked regularly. Perhaps I had acquired my father's trait of strategy. Methodically, I planned the reinstatement of my plan. Liquids could easily go down the sink. Solids would have to be disposed of in the toilet. I could not risk using the wastebasket and have someone locate the disposed food.

Six weeks had passed since my admission. The threats of continuing abuse were being voiced. If I was to succeed with my plans, I would have to do it now. If not, I feared my discharge could be an immediate return to his rapes. My only choice was death. Slowly and secretly, I had to accomplish this. Suicide was acceptable, but his rapes were not. The terror, the pain, the hate had to be resolved. If it could not be, my existence would be one of rapes, terror, physical abuse, and intense hate. If I did not die now, I would die of the intense hate I harbored against both men and women. Women, because of my mother's rejection and disbelief, and men, because of my father's rapes. There were no adults in my life or in the world that I trusted. No one was to be trusted. I thought about Nanna and wondered where she was. Life without her wasn't safe or desirable. I was only a vessel for lustful satisfaction. The existence of me was senseless. Those thoughts made my plan even more desirable. I had been raped by the man who should have protected me.

Life was not a pleasure. It was a burden, a burden so heavy at times that I thought I could smell an albatross swaying around my neck; my shoulders warm from its body heat; my heart beating rhythmically with its heart; its wings softly pressed against caged hate; its lonely call sounded as I had felt much of my life. Was it more lonely to be an albatross or me? Or did it really matter about either of us? I had valued my life as that of an albatross. And I could think of no real value of an albatross, especially so far out at sea.

Weekly weigh-ins could be a problem unless I could add weight by some means. It was impossible to stuff my pockets, but I could drink excessively before that time and if I ate only the meal before, I should be able to escape anyone's attack. The importance of my not being detected was known only to me. There was no way that anyone could understand my desired death except perhaps the albatross. I saw great sadness in the bird, much like that in my life. It was such a massive sadness that nothing else in life mattered. The consumption of the world with sadness was flashing over and over in my mind, projecting everything else as obsolete. I realized the damage my father had done to my mind. Could the damage be repaired, or should I just continue with my plan?

Ambivalence! It conflicted my soul in so very many endless ways. My mind telling me different from my heart. Acknowledging that what my heart felt was not always the most rational choice, and what my mind told me was breaking my heart. It was that conflict that propelled something in me to struggle for survival. Why? Why did something create this struggle? Adhering to the struggle's call meant that irrevocable abuse would continually be adding to the emotional damage. It was this continual struggle that caged my being in a torturous world. Perhaps I was having second thoughts about my plan, or maybe I was just scared I would fail at this also. Failure—was that why my father raped me?

Was that why my mother abandoned me? Should that have been my name? Again, questions without answers.

The plan continued. Within ten days, my weight was becoming an issue. My father was livid with anger. His daily visits were times of threats of what he could do and would do unless I immediately began to eat and maintain my weight. How I hated him and what he was doing! I wanted to die, but I did not want him anywhere around. I would continue hoping against all odds that I would succeed. If failure was once again to invade my life, I would have to find some other way that was acceptable.

Several visits from my father revealed enraged threats of distributing the pornographic materials among the adolescents in my school. This would have finished destroying me. I did not think I could live through the embarrassment of my peers. Convinced he would do precisely as he threatened, I began eating and maintaining my weight. Each day brought me closer to the day when I would be discharged into the abusive rapes of my father. It was inevitable—my father knew that—he knew the power he had over me; he knew the humiliation I had endured because of the rapes; and he knew how important it was for me to remain silent.

The long-feared day arrived. I was going home to my father. My mind did not bother to avoid thinking of what he would do at the first opportunity. Another horrible series of weeks or months until the next hospitalization that would grant me a brief reprieve.

We had been home just a few hours, when my mother departed on an out-of-town visit. That was an indicator of rapes with heavy terror. These always happened when no one else was present. All I could do was wait. The waiting, the thinking, the knowing that for the first time in three months my father was going to rape me again. His anger had already been displayed. There had been three months I had been hospitalized. Would he be more aggressive and more abusive because of the elapsed time? Would he be angry with me for being gone so long? Would he use objects to rape me? Why did I have to live just for his sexual gratification? Why did he have rights but I did not?

CHAPTER 13

There was something about the waiting that invaded all peace. If indeed, there was any peace, the waiting would destroy it each time. I had hoped to never live through this horror again. My plan, having failed, labored me with more waits. Two things were stable in my life—one, the abuse, and the other, the waiting. I had debated if death was a stable hope or not, but had decided it could not be, since I had failed at taking my own life. How I hated the abuse; his lustful dirty acts destroying me bit by bit; his nasty words forever ringing in my ears; and his memories always taking over whenever he was absent.

It was not right for him to do this to me. I wanted it stopped, but was powerless against him. My nightmares were becoming more and more real; I wanted to sleep less and less. Thoughts of murder plagued my soul, searching for one thing to make the act acceptable. That one piece of me that kept saying murder and suicide were wrong was keeping me alive for more and more torture. Why would I want to remain alive with his liberties destroying me? There were so many unanswered questions.

His appearance in my room meant one thing. I silently looked at him as his eyes plastered my body. The silent stare! Oh, how I had learned to hate the silence in him. It was invasive. Knowing I would not speak until spoken to, he would often elongate the silent time to torture me. During his silence this time, I thought of the last three months and how nice it was not to have him rape me. For the first time in years, I had lived a somewhat normal life. It was those times that made me want to live.

Was he the devil's advocate or was he the devil himself? That would certainly answer a lot of my questions, but nothing would make this acceptable or right. Being absorbed in my "why" search, I failed to note his movement toward me. His hand touching my leg startled me. Without thought, I grasped the invisible shelf and pulled myself onto it to watch the lustful sins below. The other me looked into his face only to recognize that silent smile she had learned to associate with his rapes. Slowly stroking her leg with his hand made her mind scream. She felt obligated to sit silent while his hand continued its way under her clothing, creeping closer and closer to her genitals.

Accompanying his hand were his nasty comments of old, "Daddy is glad his little girl is home again. I've missed our special times together. It's been a long time since Daddy fucked his little girl. You know what Daddy wants. You want it, too. It makes us both feel good. It's just you and me tonight, unless you want more. All Daddy has to do is call them. They'll be here real fast. You want more than one dick tonight. I haven't fucked you in a long time."

Pushing his hands inside her panties, he forced her down onto the bed. Smiling, he shoved his fingers inside of her as the other hand loosened her shirt. His arousal was obvious; time was creeping in on the silenced victim. Taking his penis in one hand, he shook it in her face. Grabbing from her the last few pieces of clothing, he dropped his trousers.

She wrapped her arms around her chest and tried to stitch her legs as one, but he overpowered her. His mouth roamed wildly about her chest. Her body trembled as he forced her legs apart. Laughing loudly, he said, "Daddy's big dick is going up inside you. I want to make you bleed again.

I like that." His penis felt like a knife entering her. The thrusting back and forth bruised her stomach. Each time he pushed inward, sharp pains radiated throughout her abdomen. It appeared the pain brought him great pleasure. His painful sucking, pulling, and biting of her breasts indicated his orgasm was near completion. She had associated this with the greatly enhanced wetness between her legs.

She knew that he would leave shortly. As she looked forward to that, his intense thrusting movement captured her attention as he forced more and more of his penis inside her. His arms had moved under her back with his hands clasped over her shoulders giving him more leverage as he raped her. Those sad eyes looked up as if pleading to God for this to end quickly. Her body cried with pain, disgust, embarrassment. His penis striking her internal organs forced the outward screams of pain. Upon completion of his orgasm, he grabbed her face, reminding her that any screams should be for continuance and praise of his act. Letting go of her face, he slapped her violently.

With crushed spirit and closed eyes, the other me fell against the bed, thinking he was gone. Much to her dismay, he returned to stand directly over her face, uttering, "Clean Daddy's dick with your tongue."

When she hesitated, he shouted, "Now!" His orders were followed.

Within several minutes, he cupped her chin with his hand, focusing her eyes upon his face. He ordered, "Lie down."

His request was for oral sex to commence and end upon his instruction. With fists held high, she followed his instructions. His mouth went to her genitals perhaps out of spite more than anything else. He knew she was appalled with all of this, but continued. His penis was growing inside her mouth. She could feel his tongue. She tried to wiggle away, but his hands grabbed her buttocks, pulling her closer as he became more aggressive.

Quickly and without notice, he halted his actions. The other me was bewildered, but also relieved. It was over. She could once again merge with the others. As she began this walk back across the bridge, gauging this gap, she heard him say, "I think you need some more practice." The other me was destroyed. Leaving the invisible shelf, I went to the aid of her, lying in a lifeless heap, exhausted from the ordeal.

The cognitive me made an immediate internal thought of pain—him, his guests, me. It was once again the hunter and the prey. The prey outnumbered and powerless before the hunters. My mind rambled on, thinking how it must be for deer during the hunting season, always wondering if the hunters were there and yet knowing their weapons could destroy them. What a most unpleasant feeling. I would not be physically destroyed, but would be brutally raped over and over. The result, caged hate growing more and more and more! A hate so enraged passively that my being yearned for death, a sure farewell to life.

Hours had passed since my father's departure. The evening was present and progressing, which could only mean his guests would be arriving soon. The helplessness of this wait was reinforced by the silence of the house. Too tired to think, I felt myself in that trance state between awakening and sleep. The world was here, but dimly; the sounds were present, but muffled; I was in the bed with that protective barrier surrounding. I could let my mind rest for now. It could take a temporary escape from his lust.

When he was ready for me, he would come to my room. Until then, I wanted to be alone. My mind would not torment me with the thoughts of the coming events, but rather nurture me, as it was my only source. Probably that was why I survived year after year. I nurtured myself as parents should, never knowing if what I did was correct or not. The knowledge of what life should be is what nurtured me, knowing that the horror would pass day after day. It would comfort me once again before, during, and after. This made survival an actuality.

The sound of the door brought me back to reality. The trance had met closure. The time piece was once again in place. The keeper of the time was my father. Only he would decide if this would be a slow or a fast pace. Either choice produced the same result. The hunt had commenced.

Standing in my door, my rapist stared at me. The silence! Time moves so slowly when one is uncomfortable. He walked over to the bed and sat down.

His words were simple, "It would be to your advantage to remember what you are afraid of, what you don't like. Do not disobey me!" His message was clear, whatever was suggested, requested, or fulfilled, he expected me to be a willing participant.

Life and living were morbid thoughts. Three months had been spent restoring and maintaining my weight to keep me alive. And this is what it was for? The ones who interfered with my suicide plan were the ones who would benefit from my life. Insurable interest—both of them were dependent upon my survival. Had I died, my father would have to find someone else to rape and rape and rape. My mother had the perfect substitute for her sexual role. It was not my death they fought to prevent, but rather, the discontinuance of my being available for their sexual avoidances and gratifications. It almost seemed that there should be a law against procreating for this purpose.

Bits and pieces of conversation floated into my hearing zone. My father was en route for me. What would he request or, rather, demand of me? How many were there? The anticipated pain was rising. A glance in the mirror revealed the dreaded moment. Instructions were clear and precise, "Please join us." No chance of misconstruing his deadly message. Without hesitation, I joined them, knowing that, if I did not, there would be too much pain for me. There were no clues at this point as to what would be occurring. My entrance into the room brought silence and glaring eyes. Whatever had been discussed prior to my entrance was unknown. Apprehensive regarding the men, I stood unresponsive. Searching my mind for my invisible shelf, I located it and pulled myself up to securely sit beyond their grasps.

She just stood there as hands reached out and mouths began to drool. Standing still, her father proudly displayed her to his seven guests, clearly stating their needs would be met. She didn't know these men, and from their conversation, they weren't friends of the family. They appeared to be out of their environment with the paintings and furniture. All the men were drinking as they walked around staring at her. One walked up and exposed her bra forcing her to back away. Her father stepped behind her reminding her to be "nice" to his guests. Upon his instruction, one of the men removed her bra and one removed her skirt. The hands and mouths were repulsive as they pawed and whistled at the frightened, unwilling soul. Her father laughed, ordering a halt to the action.

Organization! That was what he said they needed. With organization, he assured his guests everyone would be satisfied. As each man made known his desire for sex, she was to honor them regardless. As the demands increased, her body was tired and bruised, but she was not allowed to stop. Much hatred was caged that night for the exploitation he had initiated. The physical and emotional damage resultant of his sexual pleasures were never noted by him. He seemed to believe without a doubt that this was an expected behavior; that he should be teaching sex in this manner.

That night was worse in so many ways that the other me had difficulty in thinking about them. These would have to be saved for another day. This other me could not endure, and leaving the shelf from high above, I realized some things are better not remembered.

I was caught up in my thinking again, making it through another brutal night of forced sex. My father did not participate with the group, leaving me to think he would rape me later when everyone was gone. How could he allow this? And why should he watch these other men raping me? Did he enjoy this? Did he receive some satisfaction in doing this? Was he punishing me? Within all of these unsureties, I was feeling more and more dirty and wanted more and more to die.

The men were getting fulfilled, with many going for the alcohol versus me. The events would soon end, granting me a reprieve. I so much wanted a long, hot shower washing the filth from my skin. I wanted to feel cleaner. I wanted to be far, far away from the dirtiness of my father. I wanted to be forever alone some great distance from here, where dreams aren't invaded by lustful memories and where one's dreams can come true. How I wanted all of this to end!

Abruptly, my father turned to me and said, "Go upstairs and take a shower."

As I was walking out, I heard him say, "She's my private whore. Whenever I want her, I take her. A man my age needs a good fuck a day."

I climbed the stairs and hurried into the shower, where the water would wash away the smell, the body fluids and, temporarily, the memories. I was very tired. I prayed that I might sleep without flashbacks.

CHAPTER 14

The crate was always, always there, empty, seemingly without purpose. I can't ever remember anything being shipped in it. It seemed to just appear one day in the basement. With no labels and no writing, it looked new, not used. Its presence created eerie vibrations. Perhaps I sensed the danger long before it became a part of his rituals. It was large enough for a person to climb into, but not much room to move about. My mind entertained the thought, but relinquished it as the closure of the lid imaged in my mental eye. Just that fleeting thought made it difficult for me to breathe; my body shook, my skin covered with a cold sweat. The crate evoked nightmares too real to withstand. It was enough to make me yearn to be far away.

Seldom did I go into the basement. It was such a frightening place with its darkened and damp air so cool to the senses. Why I was there that day was hard to recall. In search of some item, the luring power of the crate became my focused attention. This compelling urgency of the absorption emitted found me lost in time. Startled by his footsteps, I became uncomfortable, afraid of doing some small act that would provoke his anger or not doing what he wanted me to do. There was no way to win with him. His note of my anxiety regarding the crate created an urgent need in me to flee.

Once in my bedroom, I was more comfortable. At least in this room, I knew what would happen. I had always survived that terror. But the basement and the crate held the possibility of tortures I could not endure. It was one of my fears—being shut inside a small area. The idea alone imaged such a realistic reaction I was unable to think clearly. He knew he could use it against me. The idea had already entered my mind resting there conjuring up the anxieties and fears. Shaking my head, I put the thoughts away. They could rest until I could manage their impact.

It was Friday afternoon, late afternoon. The usual trip for the weekend had not begun. They were routine by now. Hate originators. I had given that name to them because of their negativity. They were shocking and demoralizing, but always short of death.

His appearance at my door unnerved me. He chuckled as he said, "Does my crate upset you?"

It was a rhetorical question. A statement to affirm my thinking. He knew he was right. There was no need for my affirmation. If anyone was close to knowing me, it was he. It was that knowledge and how I thought that became his greatest weapon in maintaining control of me. Without control, his abuse would have ended. The crate had, however, given him one more advantage in this battle.

The dread of the rituals was stirring in my head. I wanted so much to be left alone. I wanted him out of my life. I wanted him dead. Death! His, or *mine*, would bring closure to this nightmare. The thoughts of killing him developed a plan. But, somehow, I just couldn't do it. I think it was the blood. Its sight and its peculiar odor, one I could detect immediately. Perhaps fate would destroy him for me. Things seemed to work out for others, why not me? My only other option was to wait it out. Survive moment to moment to moment.

He stood there watching. How I hated that! His watching as I labored with his dreadful lust. Slowly, he was destroying me. Surviving another attack from him was incomprehensible. I wanted to be clean. Something I could not feel when close to him. Distance! I needed distance. I needed shielding from his abuse. But where was my refuge? His departure went unnoticed, but I did sense his eyes no longer beaming down upon me. I breathed easier. My mind could relax briefly, but not for long. I was tired of thinking. There were no solutions within my control.

Suddenly, I felt his eyes on me again. That weird feeling when someone's eyeballs have plastered themselves onto your skin refusing to budge. Oh, God! I had to think again. His glazed stare was already present. We were still in the city. We hadn't driven to the lakehouse. That meant one thing. He was going to rape me here. The crate imaged itself within my mind. Surely, he wouldn't use that to torture me. I would do anything to avoid being shut away in such a small space. He knew that. This was not going to be the usual rituals.

Almost gleefully, he announced we would be staying home for the weekend. Walking over to me, his hands went inside my clothing. His excitement was pronounced as he said, "Daddy's going to have a man over to help us tonight. You know what I expect. You be nice to him."

Oh, how I had learned to hate, to despise men, to plan actions I would not have before. My legs were weak. My head had a lightness to it. Psychologically, I was torn between wanting time to stand still and wanting time to quickly pass so all his lustful abuse would be over. Both wants equally balanced. I wanted to scream at him, to order him to begin, to hurt him, to kill him. But none of these wants was acceptable. Like feathers on a bird, I was stuck in his passion. I needed a shower to wash his glances from my body. I promised myself a long cleansing one as soon as he left.

Harbored inside my head were the anxieties of my father. They were jammed into every crevice and every fold.

There were so many of them, they must have overlapped. Could there be more? Could some of them be quieted? Or could some be carefully tucked away? Could anything be forgotten? The water was reassuring, forming that barrier between him and my skin. I was clean when it was present. I was lovable. I was a person with value, no longer tainted. I was human, a whole person again. My haven had provided me shelter from intense memories of him. It was collaborative with my created world. A world where the abuse was quickly pushed away. A world where dreams would someday open the door to a normal life. A world where I wanted to live, such a great contrast to the real world where much of my time was focused on death. My fantasy world gave me the chance that wasn't available in the real world. The chance of being loved as a parent would love a child. Realizing this chance would never actualize forced the turning off of the water. Stepping out of the shower, I wanted the rituals over with as soon as possible.

Conversation drifted up the stairs. His guest had arrived. My dread of the evening would soon be quieted. My calmness was surprising. Usually a high level of panic was visible, but not tonight. Perhaps I was getting acclimated to his rituals, or maybe I had just grown indifferent. Whatever the basis, my mood was not important. It wasn't important because I wasn't important. Rather, not important for my well being. Their voices were getting closer. I heard footsteps on the stairs. Looking toward the door, I saw my father and his guest. No introduction, just two wicked stares. Who was this other man? Why was he here? What had my father planned?

Walking down the corridor, they entered my father's bedroom. That familiar churning was already present in my stomach. I realized then what a horrible home this had become. I tried not to think of the present situation. Internally, I was hoping he would not want me included. That was stupid! Of course he did. That was his delight. Without notice, a hand touched my face. My heart sank!

Pulling me up from the bed, he softly said, "We'd like for you to join us."

Without speaking, I proceeded to walk through the door. He stopped me. I turned to see why, only to hear him say, "You won't need your clothes. Take them off here."

Speechless, I stood there as he undressed me. Leaning down, he put his mouth on my breasts. His facial expression brightened. Putting his body behind mine, he pushed me into his bedroom. Lying on his bed nude was his guest. He smiled as he looked at my body. My father undressed and joined him.

I was still standing when I felt the floating sensation associated with the invisible shelf. I was safe now, able to look down upon the other me, knowing only horror was to prevail.

He pulled her onto the bed. Each began kissing on her breasts, seeming to go on forever. Her father stopped and left the room as his guest moved his mouth to her genitals. She tried repeatedly to push him away. But her father returned, laughing. He held her hands instructing his guest to "go on and have some fun, I can get this anytime."

Placing his knees on each side of her head, he pushed his penis into her mouth. His guest, pawing at her breasts, entered his penis. The sounds of that evening are forever etched within her memory. Her father having oral sex and his guest having vaginal sex. They hurt much, much more deeply than before. Disgust filled the other me. Pain had gone away long, long ago. Now, only the dirtiness and the disgust remained. It was time to leave the shelf to mend this other me, to put her back into storage.

This was a short ritual, which meant one of two things. They were tired, or they had more plans for the evening. My second choice was correct. They had simply tantalized their appetites. They would rest for a while before returning.

I cringed at the terrorism my father's perverted mind could conjure. Anything bizarre seemed to arouse him. He had tried a large array of techniques and methods. Somehow, I knew he could think of something before the evening was over. And, if by chance he could not, a repeat of some of his prior bizarre behaviors would suffice. I shouldn't really have been surprised. He had done just about everything. I showered again in an effort to push away their lust.

Hearing the door open, I glanced in the mirror to see my father with his demanding stare. They were ready to begin. "You can take those clothes off." he said coldly.

Without looking at him, I said, "Please don't hurt me anymore. I don't like doing this."

Grabbing my arm, he shouted, "How can anybody fuck you while you have clothes on, bitch?" Taking my clothes from me, he walked out, ordering me to follow.

My mind could not process living through this hell again. I hated walking around nude for his amusement. Approaching the stairs, I screamed, "No!"

Shocked at my noncompliance, he stood forever, looking at me. I saw the fury in his eyes as he covered the two steps separating us. I stepped back. With all the force he could gather, he shoved me down the stairs. As I rolled and tumbled through the air, I prayed I would die. Landing at the bottom of the stairs, he pulled me off the floor, laughing in my face. There was still fury in his soul.

I regretted resisting him. I thought of the crate. And somehow, he read my mind. Pushing and shoving, he made our way to the basement. Screaming obscenities, he threatened to put me in the crate and leave me. I was speechless. I did not want to go into that crate for any reason. I suppose I was in deep thought, or fear, and didn't see the anger building. All I heard were his words shouting in my ears, "I'm going to kill you!"

He pushed me away before grabbing the lid of the crate. I ran for the stairs. I didn't look back. Then, just when I thought I was free, his hands hit heavily upon my shoulders. Oh, the dread of the feeling as the world is crushed by the one person you fear most.

Dragging me across the floor, I floated back to my shelf away from his anger. The other me was facing death. Picking her up, he dropped her into the crate. Her terrified screams begging him to let her out only provoked his laughter. Her mind at the height of fright could see him laughing. She had never been so frightened. When he took a few steps away from the crate, she anticipated his departure.

Laughing hysterically, he lunged at her. Grabbing a handful of nails and a hammer, he shut the light out. The pounding of the nails echoed the vibrations in her head. The lid to the crate was nailed shut. Oh, how dreadful that fear in total darkness! Unable to breathe, her head hurt! Her chest felt the pressure from the small space as the sides moved in closer and closer! Her fingers felt tingly; there was numbness; and then, she fell, in slow motion, forming a lifeless heap on the floor of the crate.

Suddenly, the shrill pitch of nails forced through wood aroused her thinking. He was prying off the lid. There would be light. Breathing would be easier, and maybe he would let her out. A breath of cool air floated down upon her as her eyes grasped the first rays of light. He indicated for her to stand up, but her legs were too weak. Helping her out of the crate, he was totally silent as he rubbed his hands on her breasts and buttocks. He simply looked at her as she moved as far away from the crate as possible.

Walking past him, she was reminded how she could stay out of the crate. All she had to do was to entertain the two of them. Upon his departure, I comforted the other me, cradling her head until the pain subsided, allowing us to rejoin.

This wasn't one of those times people grit their teeth and plunge forward. There was no desire for what they wanted. His primary goal was for me to enjoy sex with him, but he had been unable to fully involve me in the act. More specifically, my body had not responded to his sexually. Once that occurred, he believed sex would be enjoyable, and I, in turn, would beg for that time with him.

As the evening passed, their pleasures were fulfilled, and with that fulfillment went another chunk of me. There were so many chunks missing—chunks of humiliation during hours of abusive terror. Always chipping away at me, he invested extraordinary thought and time in his lustful self. It was his priority. He was so consumed with lust. It is sad to have part of you strewn somewhere along the way. It's like a little piece of you dying each time. I tried to think how to retrieve those departed chunks. I could not find them. They were in a land somewhere far away and I could not get there.

CHAPTER 15

Years have passed since the initial abuse. Rarely, now, did I ever think there would be an end to my nightmare. Tonight would be another of those that chiseled away at my total self. A night when only death would be a viable solutior with an impossible probability. The mind was incapable of imaging the approaching chain of events. My fearful desire of total destruction had never actualized. Instead, the terror only maximized with unlimited boundaries, with myself as its battlefield.

His cold, silent stare frightfully reminded me of those nights when his familiar terror filled the hours of darkness. With his constant controlling spell intended not to kill, but rather to debase and destroy bit by bit. Experientially, I had learned the specifics that heightened my father's anger. Resistance and noncompliance ranked second only to weight. Each pound added intensified the anticipation of the expected rituals. Rituals from which I always emerged as a wounded player.

Fearful my father would notice my increased weight, I avoided his presence as long as possible. His subtle appearance indicated it would only be a matter of time before he would know. Without speaking, he took my hand and walked me through the house. Immediately, I knew where he was taking me and why. I also knew his anger would be highly volatile. Nervously, I awaited my destiny. He had always found my physical size compatible with his sexual desires. This thought dwelled upon my mind during the drive. Around every corner and through each bend, I realized I had no option. Dreadful hate exploded within the loathsome memories of last spring. Unfortunately, fate would once again bring me through despite my vehement opposition. Often the most painful memories were those with the silent beginnings. This was one of those times. Our quick entrance inside was followed by a rush to the bed. Laughing and chuckling, he pushed me onto it. His increasingly threatening laughter shrieked through my ears as he undressed me. The intensity of his laughter always indicated the severity of his pleasures. Tonight, the laughter and chuckling was unusually intense. My inner thoughts had no capacity to understand the moment. Efforts to learn were stumbles in ignorance.

His stare became more intense. For a long, long time, he stared at my nude body. Suddenly, harsh silence replaced his laughing and chuckling. He moved his hand slowly across my lower abdomen, several times clenching his fist with each stroke. The grinding of his teeth calmed.

Without warning, his clenched fists came crashing down upon my abdomen. Repeatedly, he struck me, shouting, "Slut! Slut!"

Each time I cried out with pain, he hit me again. He demanded to know with whom I had been sexually active. Mass confusion swelled my brain as I attempted to discern what to do or say to make a safe exit from this terror to the next.

Time's silent passage pounded through my mind. My body pained me, unbearably wrenching with each slug until this, too, came to an abrupt end. Bringing his glaring eyes close to mine, he quietly ordered, "Stand up." I hesitated.

Grasping both of my arms, he screamed, "Stand up, slut!" I followed his command.

Standing in silent fear, I watched him pace the floor, indecisive of his next move. The attempt I made to sit down provoked loud demanding shouts.

Rushing toward me, he screamed, "Stand up, slut! Stand until I see blood running down your legs!"

Time passed as I stood in painful horror. He continued to pace, looking intently for the absent blood. I inwardly prayed he would give up and leave me alone to nurture my wounded self. In a state of rage, with clenched fists, he hit me again. His force dropped me to the floor before my journey to the invisible shelf was complete.

Angrily, he dragged her to the bed with orders to undress him. The pleasure he derived from this was coupled tonight with his demands for specific sexual statements. She refused. His anger became greater and greater. Tying her hands and feet, he repeated his demands. She remained silent. His eyes ejected daggers as he finished undressing. His fists pounded away again. She was too frightened to respond. His anger continued to build.

Taking a hunting knife, he placed it between her lips, pressing firmly. With his body over hers, he spoke harshly, saying, "I'll cut your mouth all the way back to your ears if you don't do exactly what I want you to do. Now tell me what you want! Tell Daddy to fuck his little girl!" The taste of blood urged her to comply with his wishes.

Hearing those words come out of her mouth delighted him.

He responded, "That's a good girl. Now tell Daddy you want to suck his dick." She complied. His delight increased. Abruptly, his demeanor changed without taking any action on her forced requests.

He left momentarily returning with a familiar ivory object. Taking his knife, he carefully dragged its blade across her breasts. Methodically, he continued, saying, "If I ever catch you fucking around with anybody, I'll cut your nipples completely off. He won't want you after that. Then I'll cut your pussy from front to back and side to side. You won't ever feel a dick again."

He continued to laugh. He laughed loudly as he pushed an object into her rectum. His mouth roamed from breast to breast as his aggression increased. With uncontrolled laughter, he placed himself over her chest.

His voice was full of delight as he said, "Daddy's going to show his little girl what it feels like to have a dick up her ass while I eat her pussy. All you have to do is suck Daddy's big dick." Moving himself down toward her face, he pushed his penis into her mouth. Once he was sexually released, he moved quickly off the bed.

Standing above her, he began spitting in her face. His clenched fists began hitting her over and over as he screamed, "You fat-bellied bitch!" His demands to see blood continued. His anger increased as the absence of blood grew longer and longer. She followed each and every order too cowardly to force him to kill her. She prayed for his much wanted blood to appear. Again, she was alone, waiting in terror for inconceivable events. Briefly, he left the bedroom. Relief was present for just that moment.

Noises from another room grasped her attention, focusing her eyes in his direction. He was holding a large liquor bottle. There was nothing unusual about the presence of alcohol during these rituals. Only when she noticed the bottle was empty did she panic. Fear consumed her mortal soul in her mental preparation for his intrusive and brutal violations.

Laughing, he proceeded to rape her with the liquor bottle. The pain was monumental. The screams and pleas for him to stop went unheeded. Glaring at her, he stopped. His laughter erupted once again.

Picking up his knife, he shrewdly asked, "You want Daddy to stop?" There was silence.

He continued, "I'll stop your fucking around on me, you pregnant bitch! I'll show you what happens to a whore's baby. I've worked hard to keep your stomach flat. I'll cut the little bastard out!" His next move was even more shocking. It was hard to believe he would cut away at her.

She cast her eyes down upon her body, then upward. I looked down upon the other me lying in a pool of blood fresh from her. It spread hurriedly across the linens, displaying the bright redness of the life leaving her. Her head moved slowly from side to side as she focused upon visions within her range. Sounds appeared to be unimportant to her. By some strange reason, moments of silence infiltrated them. Sadly, there seemed to be much, much pain about the other me wrestling among the results of lust time and time again.

This was the end, perhaps, for his anger was being greatly intensified and directed at her. Her eyes reflected the undeniable horror silently scanning for an escape. This other me was frightened, maybe even as frightened as me, but it was irrelevant since no one would do anything to stop it. Looking down at the other me, she felt so saddened and so alone. Securely, she stayed upon her shelf knowing that soon he would hurt the other me again destroying her cell by cell.

How would it end this time; and when it was all over, how many more me's would be created? There were many times when she counted all of them to find one or two having been omitted. There wasn't time to count, maybe she could tomorrow. But for now, she had to watch the me's creation.

Often she would watch the travesties of lust. Only when the terror escalated did she yearn not to look, but always she lingered her watches, somehow giving consolation to her other me in silence.

This time it was different. It seemed this me was about

to encounter the worst of her aggressor. There was a trait about this me that had never been present before; one that seemed extremely frightened; one more eager to die than any of them; one much too defenseless, stripped and tied to his bed of lust, all alone in a dirty, dirty room. Coldness.

That was the added variable tonight. The air was cold, not just a cool feeling, but, a cold, cold encampment of life just before it ends. She understood these feelings—they were hers, not the other me. For the other me absorbed the more painful feelings, leaving her with those that she could deal with and survive. There would be no description of the emotions of the other me. She internalized the horror, somehow shelving it within the crevices until processing of its pain is possible. On that dreaded, labored night, the other me shielded me from his onslaught, making it manageable even at its highest peak.

The night also birthed the realization that the other me's were her survival routes, a small taste of freedom, a way of making it to the end. Oh, the guilt she endured for escaping the pain, for pushing the terror onto the other me's each time she failed to have enough courage to stay. It wasn't always easy to abandon the other me's. This always, always, without a doubt, brought on a familiar feeling of loneliness, as if herself had been abandoned. Why was she abandoning the me's, when they seemed to keep her from total destruction?

This me was anxious, perhaps from his pacings of the floor. His knife gleamed in the light of the room each time he flashed it through the air as it reeked of danger. These me's were very courageous to save her, but even they, at times, cringed from the brutal violations and their anticipation.

Peering down from the shelf of safety, she silently watched her other me twist in agony, bleeding profusely as he turned the knife inside her. Despite her desires, she could not bring herself to stop the thrusting of his knife. She wanted to help, but was too frightened.

And then the blood flowed heavier and heavier. The linens became drenched with her fresh blood as if muddied by a rain-drenched dog. The warmth of the blood soon changed to coolness—uncomfortable, nasty, inescapable.

She lay there for a long time, like a worm centered on a hook, helplessly restrained. The constant dull pain was intermixed with sharp excruciating jabs radiating upward into her abdomen. How she yearned to hold her stomach to ease the pain, or to curl into a ball, engulfing the wounded cells. The horror was too great—no one to help, no way to stop him, no chance of running away. Held in a time zone, her terror wasn't. It seemed the only variable with emphasis; the one that had, oddly enough, created this crazy time zone of wasted lives.

The other me was passive, almost without movement, just waiting. Or perhaps, doing nothing, weak from the spilled blood. Maybe the other me had been abandoned also, just as she. It wasn't difficult to tell, looking down upon the scene, but whatever was there within that body was quiet, from fright or from the solitude of floating somewhere about the great beyond of the universe, away from this trauma. There was a comfort in that nothing was happening at this moment, an almost contentment in the halting of his attack for however long it may be.

The stoppage of the ticking clock served temporarily as a safety net, disguising the deep invisible hole ready for her devourment. As a ship floating calmly in its harbor, the other me just existed. There was nothing to do, nothing to say, nothing to feel.

Time wasn't frozen. Rather, distorted. It had only been seconds since the knife entered her. The pain seemed as if it had always been there. The sharpest of the pains being as he twisted his knife before withdrawing it and then slamming it into her once more. His brightened, smiling face indicated he must have accomplished his intended goal.

The other me cringed as he stared at the dripping knife. Profusely, her blood poured out. Nothing could be left of her, for she could feel her insides falling out onto the linens. All the other me could think right now was how she would feel as the last of her blood seeped away. The calming silence it would bring without regard to his demands. She looked warmly through her mind's eye at the haven awaiting, already benefiting from the pleasures in store.

A numbness had spread over her mind, disallowing all but the sharp, shooting pains radiating from inside outward to the exposed tissues. She felt estranged from her environment—distorted sounds, dim lights, halting movements. There was a solemn sadness in the other me's search for another invisible shelf as an attempt to escape the destruction of the life inside of her.

For a brief time, she seemed to be accompanied on the shelf by the other me, but she could see her there below absorbing the terror. It was when the fetus was ripped from her body by his knife that the other me drifted upward leaving still another me to absorb his force.

The togetherness brought about a strange comfort between them on the shelf knowing the second other me was there alive, hurting, bleeding. The blood kept seeping outward onto the linens, its bright red so frightening to watch. That represented life, and it appeared most of her life was already out of her.

The other me was quiet, passive. She was alone on the shelf now. Perhaps the passivity of the second other me had beckoned the reuniting of the other me's. Together they might have enough strength to at least remain conscious, for there was little movement that could be endured. Retrospectively, the weakness saved her from death, for anger and frustration had consumed her soul, seeking revenge.

As he continued his assault on her, she thought of her revenge. There was a quality of sweetness about it, for now she would return his violations with the perfect and final revenge of death. Whether he wanted her death or not, it appeared it was already in process. A process which would end all accessibility to her, all the pain, all the humiliation.

She felt reflexes within her body, but her mind was far, far away. He was hurting her again, but that was tolerable because death was approachable now, not because she had initiated it, but because he had forced it upon her as if a part of him may have wanted to end the abuse, perceiving this as the best, most silent method. A thought of his methodical strategies lingered for just a second, but she found her mind too tired, so it was simply filed upon a shelf in a deep, deep crevice. Sleep was creeping over her, which she accepted, knowing this to be the end to his tyranny.

There was a coldness in her face. Her ears heard snatches of conversation. There was no need for the other me to surface. Death was too near. She could endure. For now, she would have to wait. Another man was in the room, looking at her, the blood, the tissues. The atmosphere had changed. Just a slight air of fear presented itself momentarily. Being too tired to summon the other me, she simply went to sleep, listening to the only sound in the room, her breathing.

Sometime later, I sensed movement within the room. There was conversation. My hearing caught only fragments of what the men were saying. My hands were free. Standing below me was the unfocused image of a man, probably a stranger. I feared a repeat of what my father had done. Instead, he appeared to nurture my wounds. His facial expression was sad. Blood on his clothes went unnoticed. He turned to my father and said, "I've done all I can do. Take her to a hospital fast."

He looked at me sadly. I looked at him until the darkness closed out his image. For that brief moment, I felt a sense of caring from this stranger. I knew I was dying. I felt relief creeping in with fear.

It's some time later, and the other me is back. There's been another change. A bright light was overhead. Had she died? What was this? Sleep! Just sleep until death arrives. That would be the safest thing to do if only death would answer her beckoned call. But no one would leave the other me at rest, always trying to awaken her, talking to her, telling her to keep her eyes open, wanting questions answered, telling her that everything would be okay. The invisible force moving her from lightness to darkness, from noise to silence, from freezing to scorching, from numbness to pain. It all just hurt too much.

Suddenly, a large, bright light appeared above me. There were unknown voices speaking rapidly. Someone placed something over my mouth. I pulled at it, but it remained. My hands were tied down again. Someone was talking to me. Another unknown man, dressed in a white jacket, talked softly, asking me not to fight. He wanted me to lie still and listen to what he had to say.

Softly, he said, "I'm not going to hurt you. No one is going to hurt you anymore. You have to trust me. I'm here to help you."

I remember telling him I was scared. He smiled, saying, "It's okay to be scared. You're safe with us. What's your name?" I responded. He continued, "How old are you?" I responded.

He identified himself as a doctor. He encouraged me, saying, "You're doing great, sweetheart. Hang in there with me." Several unknown people were standing around very quiet with sad faces. A lady in white had weepy eyes. Everything was moving in slow motion. The sounds were softened and distorted. The lights were growing dim. Mouths were moving, but no words were coming out. I tried to keep my eyes open, to stay aware of everything.

The sounds of the room gradually came back. The lights were dim, but present. I looked at the doctor I had assumed to be my friend, to find a most distressed look upon his face. Softly, he said, "We have to take you to surgery right away."

I was dying. I asked for a priest. He said, "I'm sorry, there isn't time. Hang in there. Don't give up on us now."

Events moved rapidly. Scenery changed and temperatures dropped. I was cold. My doctor stayed with me. Perhaps he was my comfort, my hope that life would be better. Or maybe just a nice safe person to be present as I died.

The other me just gave into their plans. It wouldn't really matter anyway, since the locus of control was apparently not within the other me. Perhaps this was what death was like, just another experience involving people who transported the dead to their final resting place. That was the coldness getting worse—preservation of the dead. Death was about to conquer again if time would only allow.

Confused, the other me just wanted to sleep; wanted that part of the brain telling her to breathe, to just stop long enough for death to catch up with her. She was tired of running, of just staying a few paces ahead. She wanted it all over, and yet, that second other me in her wanted to fight, to struggle, to live. What the purpose of the second was not made known. Perhaps the second me was the splitting off, to assume the role the other me wanted so desperately to vacate.

The throbbing pain that brought me back to reality opened my eyes to the same scenery that had closed them—blood, IVs, and unknown people. My inner hope that none of this really happened quickly ended. I wondered where my father was and where I was. I felt scared. I wanted to be left alone. I wanted to die quickly. I felt bombarded by questions and examinations. Detectives questioned me. I was too frightened to answer their questions.

Days later, my father came in with the same detectives. As he answered their questions, I listened. Both detectives were watching me as he told what happened. I was scared, and when he asked me to verify my father's story, I simply agreed. My father haughtily left the room. The detectives remained, telling me they questioned the validity of my father's story. They also believed he performed the abortion. I was too scared to talk.

As the detective left, their words rang in my ears, "You do not have to protect this man. If there is any way we can pin this on him, we will. I sure hope you're still alive when we do." For the first time, someone had verified I was pregnant.

My surgeon visited me shortly thereafter. He was doing whatever he could to win my trust. His conversation reflected the concerns of the detectives. His face appeared quite troubled.

Standing by my bed, he calmly said, "You are the only one who can identify the person responsible for this. This is a horrible tragedy that could affect you for the rest of your life. Don't protect this person. He's very sick. I will do everything I can to protect you, but I can't do anything if you continue to refuse to talk to me."

I was too scared to trust him, despite his kindness and concern. He apologized for the beast who attacked me. I felt both comfortable and uncomfortable in his presence. Only the cruel mental images of my father deterred my speech. I wanted so much to tell him all the terror, all the pain, all the humiliation. Somehow, I felt he would believe me, but the risk was too great. What if he didn't believe me? Would he think I was crazy?

My thoughts were interrupted as his conversation continued. "I realize you're young and have been through a terrifying experience. If you prefer, I can transfer your case to a lady doctor on our staff. She's very nice. I want you to be comfortable. Because of the violence involved, I have to perform an extensive examination. I can continue; or we can have a lady complete it. Think about it. I'll be back later to talk some more. Get some rest."

Never before had anyone been concerned about what I felt. There had been many times I had simply refused to feel anything. I had forgotten how happiness and pleasure felt. I was unsure of love. But I did know terror, hatred, cowardice, failure, and aloneness. These were the components of my life. I spent the next hour trying to build enough courage to tell. My courage never arrived.

I elected not to have a change in doctors, inwardly hoping to reach a point where I could share my burdensome secrets. Never did I implicate my father as the guilty person. I always wondered what my life would have been like had I just talked. I wondered if I blocked the course of fate by willfully not participating. Courage was always a missing element, and probably the only element which could have changed my life.

My father's absence allowed time for me to think undisturbed and to attempt to build courage. Unfortunately, I knew his destructive powers had no limits. I also knew he would destroy anyone who tried to help me. There was no option available. If I talked, someone else would hurt. This way, only I would hurt. I had no hope. The realization of my never having a normal life had fixated within my thinking. My father had convinced me the physical damage he had done could never be restored. I accepted my role in life as one awaiting a slow, torturous death.

He burst through my door demanding I dress to leave. Behind him came my doctors. They advised against my discharge because further surgery was necessary. His demands for me to dress became stronger. Fearful, I dressed in the presence of everyone. My mind and body were becoming numb. My thoughts were cluttered. Walking slowly through the door, I looked at the angered faces of the doctors as one of them encouraged, "All you have to do is say he's the one. Otherwise, we can't stop him."

A sharp scream from my father compelled me to go with him. Once inside the car, I realized the grave mistake my fear had made. Pulling my clothes away, he screamed, "You won't be needing these right now." His reckless driving created fears of an accident allowing more strangers to look at my nude body. I felt weak, alone, and frightened. My mind imaged the possible acts he might choose to initiate. Time again controlled the destiny of my life.

Flashbacks were trodding heavily upon me as we entered the lakehouse. I must have not heard my father's order, for he suddenly pushed me into the wall, shouting, "Get your fat ass on the bed!" As he tied my hands and feet again, I searched for the shelf, praying God would love me enough to let me die.

I begged him not to rape me anymore. Holding a liquor bottle in one hand and the knife in the other, he asked, "Which one?" I begged him to stop. Throwing the bottle against the opposite wall, he stuck the knife in the wall above my head.

He undressed, laughing. His erect penis appeared much larger, or my fear of the anticipated pain was greatly enhanced.

Taking the knife from the wall, he shouted, "Shut up! I'll

fuck you any damn time I want to. One more scream and I'll carve your pussy out so there's nothing left to sew back next time."

I followed his orders while searching for the invisible shelf to pull myself upon once again.

As I looked down, she was still screaming within her mind, hoping he would soon be finished. He seemed to be trying to make her scream as he moved his penis from her vagina and into her rectum, commenting how both were "good as new." Just when she thought she must scream outward with pain, he returned his penis to her vagina pounding heavily until his passion exploded inside her.

She felt dirty. She knew she would never be desired by any man. Even she did not like knowing herself, but there was no escape. She hated herself for passing up her chance for freedom just hours earlier.

He moved away from her and paced the floor nude. Intermittently, he would call her name, shaking his penis at her and laughing. After what appeared to be much thinking, he started lighting candles. Chuckling, he walked to the bed. A glazed look came over his eyes. Her fears began building again as he placed candles on the nightstand.

Grabbing her breasts with his large hands, he began squeezing. His mouth went to her breasts. Laughing, he shouted, "These tits are mine. You remember that! If you ever let anybody else suck on these, I'll cut them off and mail them to the bastard. Can you remember that?" She didn't respond.

Taking his knife with one hand and squeezing her breasts with the other, he laughed loudly, saying, "These nipples look real nice, the kind men like." He cut first one, then the other, squeezing blood out of both. He continued sucking, making the blood more prevalent. She tried not to look at her breasts. She tried not to think about the blood on his face. She tried not to think of his enjoyment.

As the candles burned, he paced nude. Abruptly, he walked over to the bed. Picking up the candles, he held them above her chest. Laughing, he dropped hot wax on her breasts. It burned, and her hands were tied. Her whole body hurt so bad.

She screamed, begging him to stop. I tried to help her, but I couldn't stand the pain. I watched as she tried to move to dodge the wax. This angered him. He squeezed her breasts, dripping hot wax directly into the cuts he had made. She screamed again. He grabbed the knife and waved it in her face. There was no one to help her, not even me for I was too frightened. I was greatly saddened, for her only thought was to die as quickly as possible.

Upon his departure, I floated down from the shelf to cradle the other me, to nurture her emotions, to clean away the blood and wax. It was heavy cleaning that was needed, not just to wash away his filth and words, but somehow to try to wash away the guilt I had for forcing the other me to succumb to his lust.

CHAPTER 16

The aftermath of the abortion ignited a quality within me that had not been there previously. It appeared almost as if I had been privy to information substantial to my survival. The physical pain had subsided, leaving only the horror of the psychological pain. It would soon be five weeks since the abortion and the immediate rapes. Loneliness, anger, and guilt devoured every cell of my body. Right or wrong was not the issue. It was my father.

Confused with the rapes and the role of my rapist, I found my present life undesirable. How could any of this happen? I was sixteen years old. How could he have allowed this? Perhaps the good in this was I had not become pregnant at a much earlier age. My father knew my menstrual cycles had not begun. He never mentioned contraceptives during those years despite his sole interest being sex.

He had been gone for three weeks, but I did not know his location. My mother had left two weeks earlier. It was just me. I could walk through the house without morbid fear. It was really a nice big structure, where a family could have a wonderful time doing what normal families do. Mine was not normal. I wondered if I was.

The emotional and physical damage inflicted by his lust had sharpened the edges of our personalties, making us beings with an inability to mesh. But did we ever mesh? This disenmeshment was the key to my unhappiness. I so wanted that kind of association. Funny, wanting something one could not have was my father's way of describing the poor. He meant monetarily, but what I meant was psychologically. But then, he considered my emotional needs addressed by his attention to me. In actuality, my emotional status was decreasing more and more with the continued abuse. But he was gone for now, meaning I was safe.

Hoping to avoid a second pregnancy, I attempted to obtain contraceptives. Due to my age, I was unable to without parental notification. How could I ensure contraception when the one I needed protection from was my father? It is so hard to do the responsible thing when everyone around you are doing the irresponsible. I would have to manage this or be pregnant again. I would die before I would allow him to cut and butcher me as he had. The hopelessness I had grown to know all too well was magnified.

The abuse had been several times weekly, sometimes every day and at times, multiple rapes per day. He never decreased. The weekends were filled with lust and no sleep. No private time, for his continual raping was carved in stone now. There was no reversal. The only reprieves were the times I was hospitalized or when he was gone. He was gone very few times, always returning with more terror and more hurt.

I had no contraceptives—I feared a second pregnancy. I began to think about this constantly. Would he do the same thing as before? Would he force me to have his baby? Would he murder me? I was convinced it would happen. There was no way to prevent it, and as frequently as he raped me and allowed others, it was just a matter of time.

His arrival home was not desired. Visuals of what he would do filled my head with monumental pain. How long would I be safe before his approach? Leaving the house was out of the question. His return guaranteed the timing.

I thought how nice it had been during the weeks he was

away. No abuse, no torture, no obscenities, no performing for his guests. Life was different—exciting, fun, painless, peaceful. How I wished that could remain forever!

The remainder of the day and night passed without him invading my personal space. Fearful of his approach, I stayed out of sight and quiet. Escaping him was the thought eating at me. Pulling the covers over my head, I curled up in my bed. I was safe here—the world was pushed away. The covers prevented its return. This was the darkness that harbored safety. This was my refuge. I stayed there throughout the night and into late morning. The longer I stayed there, the safer I felt. Wanting to stay forever dwelled upon my mind. I was safe and could think of no reason for venturing out. It was just me here and that was keeping me safe.

I wondered if this was how a rabbit felt down in his burrow. That thought reminded me of the white rabbit he gave me for my seventh Easter. He painted tiny paw prints up the back walk and across the balcony to my room. When I awakened, he was sitting in my chair holding a white rabbit with a big pink ribbon tied around its neck. He made me giggle those little girl giggles. I felt so very special to him that Easter morning so long ago when he tucked Mr. Rabbit into the bed with me. I was number one to him. Everyone knew that—inclusive of my mother.

The change in his behavior was dramatic. He was not the same father as the one on that Easter morning. I was safe with that father, but not with this one. I had prayed so many times for God to reverse time and give him back to me. God didn't. And at the time, I thought God just wasn't listening, but now I see it as moral freedom and its accompanied consequences.

My thinking was interrupted by his entrance. He inquired if I intended to get out of bed today. That was unusual.

Immediately, I got out of bed. As he departed, he said, "I'd like to see you downstairs when you're dressed."

This was really odd. My mother was away and he hadn't abused me. He didn't even look at me. I hurriedly dressed and descended the stairs. Walking into his study was stressful, I didn't know if the big, deep breath I had taken was going to be enough.

He raised his head as I entered. "I have some business to take care of at the lakehouse. Pack enough clothes for yourself. You won't be in school next week. I want you with me," his monotoned voice uttered.

Confused even more, I followed his instructions. I had learned to do so because it created less pain for me. I realized that there would be no more abuse, or the abuse would be lengthy. There was no explanation. I saw the future as one of the two extremes, but failed to acknowledge any degree in between.

I had decided not to go downstairs, but force him to come upstairs. That way, I might be able to observe any other changes, especially in a room so filled with rape memories. I suspected he would begin the abuse here, if that was his plan.

Singing as he ascended the stairs, he announced his arrival. Breathing deeply, I waited. His demeanor was quite different. He wasn't demanding of me or rude. He appeared to want to treat me appropriately. For this time, I thought, perhaps the abuse would not continue. I was somewhat relieved, but not completely convinced that my theory was correct.

Driving out to the lakehouse, he hummed to himself, exchanging few words with me. He drove with great care, not the usual recklessness. I began to think my life would improve. Upon arrival, my father walked on ahead, cautioning me to be careful. Never had he done this since the abuse started again.

Walking inside, I found myself even more bewildered. Time would answer all my questions, but then, time had a way of becoming labored and lengthy. Endurance was the key. I had to endure until the passage of time revealed my father's true behavior.

The day was progressing without the usual rituals. Looking out the window, I saw my father had walked down to the lake. Part of me wanted to join him, believing that he was the earlier father I had known. I yearned to have that relationship again. But, that little voice inside of me, that something that tells you what you're thinking isn't realistic, took the opposite belief that this abuse could not just end.

Torn between my heart and mind, he projected a strong need for my companionship. At times, I thought he was dependent upon me, needing me in order to continue with life. My thinking was changing, and I wasn't sure why or if it was to my advantage.

I stood for a very long time, watching him, wondering where things went wrong and why. My thoughts of those happy times we shared were forever lost. He looked the same but behaved so differently. Who had made the mistake? Why did I now want to mend this relationship? Why did I feel so guilty? Why did I feel I was the one who made the mistake? Life was good and simple a few years earlier.

My "why" search had captured my full attention. There was no notice of his return. Walking up behind me, he placed his hand on my shoulder. I didn't know if I should expect the rape or if it really was over. I chose to do nothing until his next move. Putting his arm around me, he kissed the back of my head, commenting that he would prepare dinner. He had not done that for a very long time. It gave me hope that my nightmares just might be at a closure. I quietly observed him while reading. I wasn't convinced of anything, but my mind was relentlessly exploring the possibilities. This time I was more inclined to think positively versus negatively.

Pretending to be reading, I watched his movements about the kitchen. That's a good thing about the lakehouse. It was very informal with little seclusion except for the bedrooms. I could stay abreast of any changes he might exhibit. The uneasiness I was experiencing was unknown in the respect that now my thoughts were not, I had to merely watch, ready to react. This would be a very unusual week if he had indeed decided not to rape me anymore.

Dinner was eaten in silence. His slight change in expression was intermittently accompanied with his humming. I was careful to watch this, determined to be ready for whatever approach he chose. Thinking positively was different and felt uncomfortable. Just maybe my life was going to change. Perhaps I could trust my father once again.

The evening continued without any inappropriate behavior. In fact, three days had passed, and he was still very appropriate. I began to believe the abuse had ended and would never again happen. I was happy, but felt uncomfortable with him. We conversed about the happy times in our lives. He reminisced about my early years and special things we had done together. The tone of his voice was calming with a blended texture of gentleness. Reassuring and believable, he seemed so much like my lost hero. Could I view him as my hero? Could I forget the rapes in order to have my heart's yearning? Confusion was seeping into every cellular part of me. It was a soft kind of confusion where one need not panic. As my mind was drifting off into sleep, I felt safe with him. Whatever had provoked the abuse had apparently been reversed or eliminated.

I was awakened by the movement in my bed. It was still night time. I was disoriented. Who could this be? The laugh I heard was piercing to my soul. Oh, no! This couldn't be happening. I had started to trust him again. As his hands fell across my breasts, my mind located the invisible shelf, lifting me upon it as the other me was subdued in horror.

His hands worked rapidly as he pushed her down onto the bed. He began his passionate kissing of a defenseless body. She didn't want to believe what was happening. Pulling at her clothes, he undressed her, placing his nude body on top of hers. His nasty comments began as his penis entered her. His body was thrusting against her for a long time—too long. She tried to resist him, only to anger him into striking her with his fists. She now knew the week's agenda. His fists pounding down onto her face forced her to attempt to move away. I wanted to tell her to stop, to just lie still, and when he was finished I would attend her wounds, but she could not hear from high above.

In a fit of rage, he tied her hands and feet as he had so many times. She was tied too tight. The cords were burning into her skin. He proceeded with his rape, entering his penis forcibly. His mouth was on her breasts, sucking and pulling as she gritted her teeth.

I thought of how good the last few weeks had been and how the other me's had not been used. I thought of how we were beginning to trust him again. His aggressiveness startled my thinking. His language horrified us as he boasted of his acts, his desires, his intentions. He demanded to know what she liked him to do, and ordered her to talk nasty to him.

I remembered the trestle and how frightened the other me was at that time. I thought we could survive anything before we would allow him to do that again. Laughing, he threatened to leave her tied for the remainder of the week. I watched the other me helpless and alone. He had won our trust and violated it once again. Perhaps this was his plan from the beginning.

Holding her mouth with his hand, he ordered her to talk nasty. Making very obscene statements, she repeated each one to his satisfaction. Looking down, I recorded his every word, his every movement within my memory, realizing that his enjoyment was smothering her. She sensed a greater fear of him, of his body. The conclusion of his passion was greatly desired. When it occurred, he left her tied and alone.

Sometime later, he returned to cut the cords. No words were exchanged. No looking back as he left. The weeks without rape had tempered the fears slightly, but the memories held fast with all of their pain. Why did we think we had escaped his wicked desires? Why had we done this to ourselves? Why had we been foolish enough to believe he would stop raping us?

There was a new me being formed, obsessed with purity, but there was difficulty in molding this one. Oh, how greatly desired by the core was that purity, highly evident in the luscious smells of a newborn, whose delicate smooth skin glows of perfection. The inability to regain that status was imposing an incompleteness to this other me. She was needed. Her cleanliness was needed. With her presence, germs could be eliminated, the blood would become clear and his repulsive body fluids would no longer touch her skin.

Struggle followed struggle only to find the demise of what little foundation had been established. With certainty, this other me would be formed and molded with great complexity. But, it would have to wait for another time, another place, another rape, or perhaps, just for a ray of hope somewhere in a world of darkness.

CHAPTER 17

Dating. That was an issue never discussed. Determined to keep me for himself, I knew my father's perception of this issue. He would never permit me to be with males my age. I had stopped asking if I could socialize. My dream was to do all the things my peers were doing. Thoughts of going to a school dance or to the theater were internal battles of wanting to go, yet knowing I could not. I entertained these thoughts often, and at times, convinced myself that these were insignificant events and would be a waste of my time, a waste of my intelligence. Inwardly, I mourned for the opportunity. I formed strategy after strategy, only to have the pieces not fit or fall apart.

Football games were a regular weekly encounter. My father attended to keep a close vigil on me, prohibiting any normal interaction with my peers. There were many nights that he would become obsessed with the possibility of my being shared without his knowledge, allowing rage to surge through his body provoking irrational behavior whose target I became. No explanation of what I was doing nor why was acceptable. The attempt to explain was useless.

I had to be very careful of any males. Such a stressful thing to do, I found it almost impossible. I either hurried ahead of everyone, or I lagged behind, hoping everyone would go on ahead. That way, no one was seen with me, especially males. He was always there, keeping his watchful eye upon me.

His distorted thinking controlled every aspect of my life, becoming violent at any male interaction. Even in a group of female peers, if a male peer joined us, he would etch within my memory a terror to haunt me.

My internal battle to avoid interaction with others was forever conflicted with my persistent yearning to be normal. The fear my father would misinterpret someone's action was embossed on my memory. Nothing was stronger within my mind until the evening my fear actualized.

On that ill-fated night following the game, a lab partner stopped to ask about an assignment. Innocently, he put his arm around me in the presence of my father. The drive home was in total silence. Scared, I knew he would terrorize me tonight. Or if I was lucky, he would just rape me without his heavy terror. There was a difference in rape with terror and rape with heavy terror. Regardless, he would rape me.

Part of me had accepted the rapes with terror. The troublesome aspect was all the other things he used. My fears became weapons for his lust. My silence reinforced his rapes. The drive coming to an end signaled the onslaught. Hurriedly, I ascended the stairs to be forgotten. In just a brief moment, he appeared at my door.

The basement was our destination. I didn't know if he would rape me or not, but he would definitely threaten and terrorize. Slowly, I followed him, dreading the unknown. His turning to ensure my following made my skin crawl. He had already given me a negative attitude regarding sex and men. I was destined to hate both.

The closer we came to the basement, the higher my anxiety. Looking at the door reflected the death warrant I would yearn for before the terror ended. I would know its beginning by the violence. There was never an ending—just continual beginning after beginning. Always a constant terror, sometimes at a high intensity and sometimes at a low intensity, but always, the terror was present. There was no one to help me. Perhaps that is why I survived the ordeal—there would be no one to care if I didn't. It was me and the splittings of my core.

He turned and laughed. I breathed uneasily as I walked by him into the basement, only to feel his shoving of me. This was going to be one of those really bad times. I stood a few feet away with my back turned. I felt his hands on my shoulders, a touch of lust in a forbidden forest. A touch that repels love. A touch of evil.

I was absorbed in my disgust, when he started pulling at my clothes. Each time he pulled an article off, he reminded me of his demands. Laughing and then appearing angry, he shouted, "I don't want you talking to anybody. All boys want is to fuck. You do that with me." There was no response for I was deep within my mind climbing upon my invisible shelf.

When she was completely nude, he delineated the body parts he would sever if she chose to continue talking with males. She stood in silence. The longer the silence, the more emphasis he placed on dismembering her body. Quickly, he moved away. She wanted to flee, but was scared. She ventured closer to the door, but stopped when he turned and looked at her.

Laughing, he shouted, "Where the hell are you going?"
She responded, "Nowhere."
Laughing loudly, he said, "You damn right you're not!"
He picked up the electric saw. His look at her indicated his motives. She envisioned the saw running through her body with blood being splattered, bones cut in half, and excruciating pain. She could smell the blood, hear the bones breaking, and feel the pain as the saw cut her body. His looks were far more effective than his threats. She knew within his mind, he had the same visions.

She realized the seriousness of the evening's agenda.

Nervously, she backed into a corner as he slowly stalked her, waving the saw. It wasn't running, but the cord was in the electrical outlet. She knew that he had just run the saw for her benefit. The closer he came, the more fearful she became. Perhaps the distance would disconnect the cord. But, it didn't . . . Holding the saw at her face, he laughed.

Running his hand across her breasts, he grabbed one, demonstrating what he would cut off. She didn't know if he really would or not, but she knew she had to get away from him. He turned and walked away, allowing her just a little hope. Then, suddenly, he whirled around with the saw running and rushed toward her.

I wanted to help the other me, to scoop her up in my arms and place her close by me on the shelf of safety, but I failed. My eyes couldn't stand the scene; my heart couldn't stand the pain; but most of all, my mind couldn't handle the fear. I had to think of something else until some of this terror passed or subsided. The realization of death to the other me, to all of us, was too vivid. I failed this other me as much as I had all the others. It wasn't fair for me to abandon them, it wasn't fair for the others to have to endure the pain. I wondered if the other me's could have splittings to pass the pain onward getting it further and further away from me.

As he switched off the saw, the diminishing sound brought my eyes back to this other me as he positioned himself against her body.

He was going to rape her, but with what? The saw was in his hand. If he chose to rape her with that, she would surely die. She dreaded seeing all the blood. Ordering her to lie down on the floor, she did exactly as he said. With the saw by her head and in her visual field, he undressed himself. Little chuckles emerged as he glanced toward the saw. She did not feel safe, a fact of which he was very much aware.

She closed her eyes, only to hear him scream, "Keep

your eyes open. I want you to see me fuck you!" She opened her eyes, keeping them on him the entire time. Smiling, he raped her savagely, not once, but twice—vaginal and anal. As he concluded his passion, he moved away.

When she started to get up, his large hands shoved her down. Picking up the saw, he threatened to sever her breasts if he even suspected she was involved with anyone. She tried to defend herself. Taking his fists, he hit her, ordering silence.

His brutal description of the saw rape left visuals that she could never forget. He would separate her body into two halves, halfway to her navel to disfigure her genitals preventing a sexual life. Laughingly, he spoke of how the saw would break the pelvic bone grinding it into tiny pieces that could not be re-formed. He spoke of the bladder being completely destroyed. But, most of all, he spoke of how big the scar would be on her abdomen, making her undesirable.

Seeing him switch the saw on, she tried to prepare herself. It shouldn't take long for her to die. She wanted to scream, but her mouth wouldn't work. He looked at her, laughed, and shut the saw off.

Calmly, he moved closer to her face, saying, "If I fuck you with my saw, you won't be able to move your legs because I'll cut into your spinal cord. Then you won't ever get away from me. I'll be able to fuck you whenever I want." He looked at her for a long time before ordering her to dress. She hurriedly dressed and fled. She needed to shower. She had to shower, to wash away from her skin the remnants of him.

The shower felt good. She felt good, fresh, and untainted. She hoped he wouldn't return tonight. There was a need to think, to focus on the behaviors that had saved her for so long. With relief, she concentrated, hoping it would all end soon. Thinking of her other me's provided her with an avenue of endurance. As soon as it was over, she ran to the shower to scrub and scrub and scrub. Toweling her hair dry, she walked into her bedroom. She wanted to lie down; to pull the covers over her head; to stay safe under them, away from the world, to be left alone.

On her approach to the bed, she gasped. He had put the saw on her bed. His message was clear. Waiting outside the door, he was delighted by her shock. Smiling, he walked over to the bed, removing the saw. With his glazed look, he said, "I *will* be back later. Am I going to need this?"

Part of her wanted to say yes, but the fear of dying was too strong. She remained silent.

Walking over to her, he struck her twice. Demandingly, he ordered, "Answer me, bitch!"

Quickly, she answered.

And he would be back just as he had said. He had two areas of predictability. First, he would always rape with terror. Second, if he said he would return, he always did. We were back to the time piece with him as the timekeeper. No one knew when he would return, but he would.

Exhausted, she tried to sleep. He invaded her dreams. She had to stay awake for she just wasn't ready for her mind's dreams. Looking into a mirror, she thought how it would be if she had had different parents. Would she have been a loved child? Or would two other people have abused her also? More questions to which there were no answers.

The night was passing slowly with painful anticipation. She wanted the raping stopped, but had no leverage to do so. Who would believe her when her own mother had done nothing to stop it. She was trying to differentiate which parent she hated more, when suddenly there was movement in the room. He was back. There was no need to resist. She was ordered to undress him and begin oral sex. And she did. He stopped her after a brief time to undress her. Moving to the bed, her hatred swelled. Even her bed seemed tainted.

There was never an escape from him. He invaded her dreams and her bed. Disgust filled every inch of her being.

Once on the bed, he progressed quickly. There was no resistance. The saw was embossed on her memory. She would do anything to avoid rape with his saw. His enjoyment was heightened tonight, his aggression lessened. There were less physical bruises, but the bruises within her mind were devastating.

The me's often wondered if we reinforced his rapes by not resisting. We finally decided that everything we did, and did not do, reinforced his rapes. He knew we were standing powerless before him.

As his shadows faded away, I went to the other me caressing her broken thoughts, hoping my love for her would smooth the jagged edges, trying to remove the wrinkles so heavily creased upon a captive and frightened creature.

CHAPTER 18

I hated his bedroom, so vile with the many tracings of his being. Much like what I thought hell would be—wicked, mean, destructive, lustful. If anything other than sin was present, it had to have been dead. Even the breath leaving him was evil, something not to be breathed by others, for surely in so doing, more clones of his would be produced. Clones—devils to continue his rapes, to harass, to torture, to kill, but most of all, to torment me with his memories until long after his death.

A relentless harbor of terror was that room of threats, in a house where no one ever hugged me, loved me, prayed for me. One, perhaps, that even God did not love, for had there been love for me from Him, surely my life would have been different—less pain, some love, some peace. Maybe God was angry with me for whatever it was that I had done.

The room reeked of him. Everything about that room was his—his smell, his touch, his words, his sins. He was not deserving of being here in this house with me. He needed to be far, far away, where no one else could be touched by his vile, sick mind. His fingers needed to be cut away, leaving unbandaged nubs to decay, dripping pus and blood all about him with no one able to help. No one would want to help. His death would be slow, torturous, deliberate. It would be an undesired death, full of fear as he witnessed the ramifications of his sadistic mind.

He would watch the full demise of his kingdom of love;

he would gasp for breath as he wrenched with pain much less than that of his victim. The throbbing pain of each finger would increase, reiterating the initial pain as each was severed from those filthy hands that harass my soul eternally. His clones pulling the skin off by layers, exposing the veins and arteries to be yanked on until they dropped out of the bloody stumps at the end of his arms. They would be useless to him. They would become burdens—such heavy burdens, with no means of relief. He would have a burden so heavy and yet have no way to lighten it.

The load would increase, and that sick, sadistic mind of his would become overwhelmed, distraught, knowing there was no functionable solution to the problem. He would begin to know a little of the terror I had lived; to experience his body being taken away, leaving him powerless, battered, and forever tainted.

Pleasures and needs would be dangled at him within his grasp, but never, never would he be able to reach them, to hold them, to use them, to hope. He would look and savor, but never experience. He would dream and dream, always knowing that they were just dreams for his mind, never to pass by his violator. He would beg, plead, cry—all to no avail. There would be no one to help, no one to care, no one to love.

Death would be allowed only after the utilization of every means to torture and destroy. The only variable interrupting his continued torture would be the howlings for death—that point just before death, when nothing really matters anymore. Perhaps at that time, the eyes could be plucked as thorns from injured flesh, tossed adamantly onto the floor, and heavily pounded upon, creating that final quality of his, which I had learned so very well. Nothing—just nothing. That is what he would be—nothing.

I would at last have made him hurt and hurt; but never would he hurt as I. But he would be gone forever and ever.

It would make my life better, since his rapes and terror would not keep growing. I would not have to add more and more of these to my memory, for he would no longer do to me the many horrible acts he had previously transgressed.

All my caged hate has been harbored until now, when I feel a relentless hate and destruction for him. My mind continually sifting the memories, always finishing with minute details that add to the memories overstocking my thinking. Why did it all happen? I wanted my life as a young girl returned. That would never happen—no way my losses could be restored to me at any point in my life. It was gone—I had been cheated by the very people who were supposed to prevent such losses.

There were serpents of hatred seething inside me, colliding with the exterior wall of my body in their search for an exit, to flee on their path to violently destroy this one, forever protecting me from his touch. They bit at me and pulled on my parts, probing and looking. There are times I watch my skin, looking for their heads poking and pushing as they fight to make their exit. I know it's there deep inside of me, the kind of hate that means death—maybe even for me. For him, without a question. Maybe for others who are just present by chance.

There is a kill drive deep within me that surfaces when thoughts of him and his lust infiltrate my being, urging me to die, to overdose, to crash, to waste away until no one and no thing will ever make me sad anymore; where he and his bedroom no longer terrorize and haunt me. I need them out and cast away if, indeed, it could be done. I need the freedom that I only think about—it isn't even a dream. I just think about it, savoring what that freedom must feel like.

All of these horrible feelings are not natural. For if there was good in them at all, I would sense an avenue to disband them rather than harbor them within this mass of loneliness.

They must be released before my body ruptures, bleeding his vile clones onto the world. There needs to be death to the clones before their release or my safety is still in question. That is the key to their release; until that time, they will remain harbored within their own destructive bomb. Time's passage enhances the need for this release, which holds me captive as if a prisoner behind bars. I just did not have the courage to release the caged hate in its entirety; for in so doing, I must risk looking at me, knowing all my past and how different I am from the rest of the world.

It was his bedroom that had helped make me so different. Nights he raped and tortured me beyond sanity are stuffed permanently inside my head. Favorite pleasures for him stifled my emotional growth, creating the abnormalities within me, which have become my master. These were the times for which I wanted him to die right before my eyes. Often I visualized what it must be to see your violator brought to his knees as his passionate crimes become known to all those he had deceived. A public accounting of his actions indicting him for the horror of his violations would be needed. It would not matter if he lived in peace ever again, as one so disturbed should have great difficulty in discerning peaceful contentment from that of lust.

Every moment of each violation should be lived by him. He should have to recall the terrors and laughs, held accountable for his sharing of my being with others, for whatever his reasoning. Everyone who ever knew him should now know what he was—a rapist, a pimp, a psychopath . . . the devil. There should be nothing omitted, just as he had omitted nothing from my terror, shelved neatly within my mind, housed eternally until someone is able to teach me to trust first myself, and then others, one by one, until I am once again that happy me I remember for those few years when he wasn't my rapist, but my dad.

Many times I thought my heart would collapse as night after night he added terror with terror, destroying my love and hope in life; creating my yearning for, and the realization that death would be the only solution to his crime. His nights of lust, so ingrained in my being, shall never be forgotten. I awake with them each day, knowing and believing that no one could visualize how a father could take his child, debase that child, and then act as if nothing has happened.

I hate him for what he did and for what he was. I hate the days and nights when he tied my hands and feet for his pleasures, particularly inside his bedroom. Always, always his filth stayed within me, never allowing cleanness again. His rituals, always so important to him; the terror was never enough; always he looked for more; always he wanted my participation in his hideous crimes. He screamed at me when my body didn't respond to his saying cruel things.

His anger was growing worse and worse! He said it was my fault, that I was a "bad seed" waiting to die. He beat me because of that, withholding meals and bathroom privileges. I found no pleasure in him or in what he was doing. I wanted him far away from me. I didn't want his hands or his eyes near me.

He raped me several times before becoming violent and bringing in his snake. I begged for a shower, not a long one, just a short one. Laying his snake upon the bed, he laughed at my plea. His snake was crawling toward me. He was laughing. I wanted him dead and away from me. Suddenly, he grasped the snake shoving it into my mouth. Laughing at my horror, his penis entered me. I felt the snake move in my mouth. I hated him so much. I wanted to kill him. And if my hands had been free, I would have. The night grew so long, and he was so persistent, with the same demands, that my hatred escalated more than ever. I wanted to die. I just wanted to die.

CHAPTER 19

One of my rapist's favorite pastimes was exhibiting his nakedness. He muchly desired his skin against mine. Moments of shivers and screams inside my memory, that dreadful moment when one yearns to draw the outer body deep within, shielding his touches. The spot in the pit of the stomach that pains and wrenches when the fear of death has settled in among the remnants of the last meal. Anybody's guess which would win. It's really irrelevant—before a victory is called, more action transpires.

The touch of flesh to flesh was unacceptable, despicable. A feeling so detested! Always wanting me to touch, look, watch! That was it today—touching! Listening to the water fill the tub, I anxiously awaited his entry. Routine at this stage, his delight in this ritual was crucial—it had become a regular. Any time an act became a regular, it was crucial. He wanted me at his beckon call, always unresponsive to my needs and desires. That was his status tonight.

His demanding nature ordered me into his bathroom, where he had prepared a bath. He was repulsive. Time after time, we had gone through this—he wanted me to join him. I resisted. As his demands continued, I remained motionless. Pointing his finger at the vanity, my eyes fell upon his canvas bag. Its contents creating a slight, but steady movement.

Reluctantly, I entered the evil water surrounding a devil. This filthy water was a hellish lake filled with suds of wickedness, floating, attacking relentlessly the cellular components of the flesh. Osmosis! That was it. An absorption of his evil through my flesh.

How I wanted him dead! His destructive hands no longer grasping, yanking me back to him. His vile voice was harsh! I had missed a cue, being absorbed in my "why" search. How I wished I could shoot daggers with my eyes, bringing him to destruction. That inability made my decision—I would kill him. Somehow, I would devise a plan that was foolproof. I would be the one to laugh last and never have to hear his wicked, wicked laugh again! Looking at him simply reinforced my thinking.

Timing—that was the pivot. Wrong timing and I could find myself in the worst terror of all, or I could be the one who died. Determined to prevent the latter, I trudged forward. Unaware of my plan, he continued his enticement as he searched for the ultimate destruction of my soul. The voice inside urged the total freedom so muchly desired. The method was undecided. The need for absolution was great. No allowances for his escape from death were affordable.

His eyes were plastered on me again. I felt them. Those beady eyes much like those of shrimp—prominent and bulging. My fingers wanted to reach out and snatch them from their sockets, laughing loudly as he wrenched with pain. Often I thought how they must yearn to pop out, becoming detached and useless. Desperately, I wanted the nerve to do it, but only with a guarantee I could escape his retaliation. The fear of revenge outweighed desire, but the yearning for freedom would yield a way.

Laughter—his! It grabbed my attention which was less and less this time. Working diligently, my mind was conceptualizing all possible solutions functionable to my plan. It might take several days or weeks, but I would devise a plan. Just looking at him assured me of that. The implementation was not in question. The deficit was in the method.

His fists came crashing down on my head. Unsure of what I had done, or had not done, I surmised my whole attention needed focusing on him. It was almost over. My freedom was close, but for now I must focus on the tasks at hand.

His demeanor had changed into that part of him that wasn't looking for sexual gratification but rather the cruel screaming of debasements. Without a doubt, he would not rape me this time, but he would say things that I would remember forever. The names he called me and the expression as he was doing so created a significant reinforcement for his reasoning behind the abuse—all the abuse, not just the sexual. Shattering statements of my need for his abuse and my desire for him sexually increased.

Later, I recognized this as one of the times when he was searching for justification of his actions. Always, always, these times ended with him telling me why I was a whore, a slut, a vessel for his lust. This was less abusive than most times physically, but most devastating emotionally. This kind of pain would stay much longer than the physical pain, but endurable with my present plan. This was one time he could not read my thoughts.

My reprieve from the tub was unexpected, but welcomed. Away to my haven to cleanse his filth from me. Standing under the water scrubbing, I thought of drowning him but ruled that out due to his physical size—too risky. I needed a plan that would be fast and successful. There were guns in the house, but I knew nothing about them, which ruled that out. Knives focused in my mind. I could attack while he was sleeping, cut an artery and let him bleed until death took over. Images of the knife as it sliced into his flesh terrorized me. Whatever the method, it needed to be distanced from me physically or I would simply be trading one trauma for another. The coldness of the shower brought me back to the present. Shutting off the water as I moved out of the shower, my wet hand touched the light switch producing a slight electrical shock. That was it! A fast, simple, and distanced plan. His lingering embellished with his wicked laugh that would laugh one last time. It would stop abruptly as he saw me toss the still connected radio into his bath water. I wanted him to see what I was doing to him. He would know his death would be immediate and successful. I wanted that—a necessary element as my mind entertained a taste for revenge.

Days passed until I gathered enough courage that I thought I could do it. I wondered what he would look like after electricity shot through his body. I wanted it to be painful; to shake his body violently; to send excruciating pains through his head; to pierce and rupture every organ of his vile, vile body. I wanted his skin burned and darkened to a crisp; and then he could die, being forever removed from my life.

Rehearsal after rehearsal had worked out each and every minute detail until it was perfected, giving me the reinforcement that I could indeed murder him, make it look like an accident, and obtain my freedom. It would close the door on so many horrors. Now, all I needed was the circumstances to avail themselves. It appeared so simple, so sure, so absolute to my survival.

The opportunities were several when I could have done it. Each time panic struck, and I was too frightened to follow through. In my meticulous planning, I had omitted a very important element that I had assumed the abuse had automatically driven into the soul of my being. Never did I think my own conscience would be the failing element to my freedom.

For some reason unknown to me even today, I was unable to murder my father, my terrorist, my rapist. I thought of all the horrible pain I had endured. I acknowledged that this would end the most devastating aspect of my life. But I just simply could not bring myself to kill. I knew I would continue to be abused until his death. But at that time, I viewed this murder plan as the only avenue to right what he had done in the name of love and parenthood. It would be many years later before I realized nothing could right the wrong and not everyone can kill, even when it means advancing one's life into safety.

CHAPTER 20

The secret my father and I shared has left memories of horror in every corner of my life. Scars which feel irreparable. Stimuli provoke memories plagued with pain and disgust as his abuse crossed over into every facet of my life—inclusive of my faith in God. As a Roman Catholic, confession was a part of my environment. Many times he must have pondered what I confessed was and if his secret was still safe. His mind had to have always planned and calculated his actions, always congratulating himself for his conquests.

Perhaps it was at these times he increased the terror, out of fear his secret was known. That *was* his one fear. I surmised he had that little bit of doubt that comes with the unknown whenever he thought of the abuse. When my mother chose to look the other way, she gave consent for the abuse. I didn't think anyone would believe me. She allowed him to successfully escape being revealed.

Confession was a regularly scheduled activity. That was the one area he would have to gain control over in order to continue his secret abuse. I was well versed in the rituals of the church, including confession. It was the only time I truly felt safe. These were times when he would not bother me, but I remember confession being emphasized to the extremes. It served as a haven much like the shower.

Several times I had attempted to tell what my father was doing, but lost my nerve. I even started verbalizing that confession only to panic once again into silence. I was torn between the priest not believing me and believing me to the point of trying to get me to a safe place. I feared what my father would do if I did tell. Those horrible crimes he had committed and those that he had threatened sealed my lips. How I wished now that I had said something to the priest. Even if he had not believed me, maybe he could have had someone talk with me who would. I always seemed to find myself at these crossroads forever haunting me regardless of my choice.

I had already acknowledged that my telling of the abuse was not an option. My father had not. His latest strategy was skillfully designed to prevent my confessing to the priest. It was unusual for my father to grill me on what I confessed. I first noticed this on a Friday evening when he had taken me to the lakehouse.

Never had he played priest with me. Never had he questioned me about my confessions. Retrospectively, I think he must have had doubts regarding the secrecy and needed to reinforce his belief. If he could control my confessions, he could keep his secret sealed. Now, on a regular basis, he would play priest, putting words in my mouth, selecting which sin I was to confess on any given day, and ensuring his liberties with me would not be interrupted.

I always felt guilty about my confessions, the uncomfortableness of the sins he chose. The anger when he abused me, forcing me into a self-destructive pattern. The devastation I endured because of his sexual lust. The loss of trust I had in the only parent that I thought loved me at one time. The confusion I experienced when he worded my confession with lies, knowing he did not confess his sins.

I questioned what God must think about all of this. I wondered where God was and how much time I would have to endure before he would provide a safe refuge. I was bewildered that the abuse was so easily accepted by my parents. Retrospectively, my mother would simply pass her role onto me whenever it was deemed appropriate by them. I did not know if this was the case, but all the variables fit.

The playing of priest was difficult for me but seemed to add a quality of appropriateness for him to an act which should not have occurred. I surmised this from the practiced confessions, which allowed him to accept himself and what he was doing. Regardless, it had become a part of our rituals. It was this preparation which destroyed that part of me I thought was still intact. The idea that parents should set good examples for their children just did not balance with what he was doing and having me do. It did not seem right for him to use the church for his sexual lust. It just seemed he had invaded too many components of life and too many other lifestyles.

Thinking of the abuse, I am uncertain which aspect was more damaging. The actual abuse was devastating. His manipulations were also destructive. The use of the church brings about strong feelings of disgust. It's hard to imagine anything more destructive than my father. It was difficult to separate any one aspect of my abuse. All of the actions appeared to feed upon one another, disallowing the separation of acts.

Many times I have pondered the particulars of my abuse. The cruelty and the number of individuals involved chips away at what remains of me. Today, confession brings flashbacks of the threats he issued if I confessed the abuse. He emphasized that if anyone had committed a sin, it was I. My sin being that I did not voluntarily participate, but made him spend too much time enforcing sex. This should have been a willful and loving labor to show my respect for my father.

Much of my time was spent confessing my failure to honor my father as he delineated. I failed to understand why all the force, pain, and terror was used if this was the normal act for a father to perform with his daughter. So many times things were not adding up, yet there was nothing I could do to resolve the issue.

Staying quiet was forced on me. The consequences for telling were too great. There had been countless threats of how he would cut out my tongue, making me a mute if I made the mistake of telling the priest or anyone else. Always he would remind me that my own mother did not believe me and no one else would either.

I attempted to dispute his word on one occasion, provoking him into a horrifying rage during which he flashed his hunting knife in my face, ordering me to "stick out" my tongue. When I did not, he cut my upper lip, allowing the blood to fall into my mouth. The taste of blood forced me to open my mouth and stick out my tongue. Using a soiled cloth which burned my cut lip, he pulled on my tongue; painfully, I could feel his knife dragging across it. I could feel blood in my mind. I imagined my tongue being cut out. The reinforcing element was my cut lip. I was unable to think clearly or with enough depth to realize the removal of my tongue would interfere with his sexual fulfillment. Oh, how I wished I had thought of that at the time. Perhaps if I had opposed him more assertively, he would have stopped.

CHAPTER 21

The partially formed other me intruded upon my thoughts, prying through the files placed within the crevices of my mind, searching for the components needed in finishing what she would be and her specific duties along this route of survival. I watched her closely from the shelf, within my mind, having been frightened there when her intense search of the past violations began unraveling my senses. I couldn't bear to relive the violations today; and when my mind refused to let them rest, this partially formed other me came to my rescue. Safely upon my refuge, I watched through her mind as file after file was sifted and resifted, as if looking for something different this time. Perhaps, she would find it.

Blood, lust, odors! The mingling of all three within her mind increased her emotions. It would seem she would be better able to deal with these at this point in her life, having been exposed and utilized year after year. Funny how one just cannot get acclimated to that which is perceived as aversive. He had made her this way, using her for himself and his chosen guests. Always, always, stealing sex over and over, knowing it was wrong, but refusing to stop.

Her body reeked of the lustful sins cast upon her, emoting filth from it all. The tainted skin plastered eternally onto her skeleton, forever trapping the savage remnants of lust. Cleaning was vital, if possible. She seemed too dirty to be cleaned, to be pure once again. The filth made breathing difficult, giving that crushing pain across the chest, like when the heart has been shattered to bits.

The filth was building, intensifying; the smells were stifling, forming pools of stagnated scum within her mind, overcoming those few memories of good times which from time to time tried to emit pastel shades of hope. It was the losing of those little glimmers of solitude that advanced another of the many me's to rescue her from this hell. Drifting away and into the air, the other me stepped forward, sealed in plastic as close to the skin as possible. There was no air or filth on her skin now, for within her mind, and in the other me, she scrubbed filth until the skin was washed away. Then, very carefully, she put the plastic on the pure flesh to seal out the lust that was approaching.

She watched the other me closely as she became a plastic form, like a doll without a breath. No life visible, but somehow there. There was an added precaution against the filth both within her mind and on her body. Carefully she slipped plastic gloves over her hands, just by chance they should touch him. The other me pulled them snugly up her arms, waiting for the attack.

This had become her practice—to reinforce her plastic seal. There wasn't an opening about her, and he despised plastic on anything. If he felt the plastic, he would leave her alone, and if he did not, the plastic would form the needed barrier between him and her. When he was finished, a new plastic seal would be put in place with new gloves freshly reestablishing her saving barrier. This other me was molding the foundation for escaping this wretched house of horror, for escaping the perpetrators of terror. But it would be one to stay forever, investing time and energy into rituals of cleaning and recleaning and recleaning.

The shower had become the nesting place for this me, as the fresh water falling upon the skin was a feeling of newness that somehow the filth of raw lust could be removed. But the memories conflicted the thoughts, making it appear necessary to scrub harder and harder. And for a while it did work, making this other me actualize when the filth was nearby. So she continued the scrubbings day after day, never allowing the remnants of raw lust to accrue. Strange how the mind allows entertainment of the facts in distortion to pacify the fears. The smells and filth of his lust were not a part of her all the time. But inside her mind, they were always there. It was vital that she be cleaned over and over. When the need for more cleaning became apparent, this other me turned her cleaning to the environment, scrubbing all surfaces with small brushes—toothbrushes—forcing a thorough inspection of every inch. This ritual helped, but most of all, it added stability in a whirling, vicious world.

Water shrivels the skin into a human prune as it purifies the cells, relinquishing those evidential remains enmeshed with a consortium of personalities straining to be free and expressive, and yet, its housing force continually strains to keep the many me's subdued. Cleaning was vital, necessary to control all of them. And now that she was older, it was a responsibility to maintain the members of this hierarchy, placing them silently and discreetly within the confines of the mind, eternally scrubbed and scrubbed until their outward cries are quieted.

Quieting—that was it—putting the many me's down for a long nap, with hopes of never having to awaken them again. She wished for them an eternal nap, for in so doing, the past would not return to her so frequently. Perhaps, never, sealing them away from her mind, and that might somehow seal the damaged layers within, closing the door to this travesty forever. Her mind did this almost always now—going off on tangents, desperately searching for a method of erasing the trauma. Denial! Yes, she worked very hard at forgetting, at wishing, at creating. That was the origin of this me.

She wasn't just clean. She was the cleanest anyone could be as long as the plastic was in place. His touches were tolerable this way, and while the other me absorbed his violations, she continued to yearn for a way out. It was more frequent now that the other me had to adorn her plastic suit, enduring the horror until at last the plastic could be discarded and the skin scrubbed and rescrubbed with lengthy standings under the waters, forbidding the wicked, lustful remnants to come in contact with her skin once she had scrubbed them away. Standing on towels while showering, to form a wall of resistance should the lust remnants escape the drain by hiding under her feet or between her toes. Her goal was to be clean at any cost to herself.

That's why the bleeding was so important each and every time. It was difficult distinguishing whose blood was being washed down the drain—his or the other me's. To ensure that none of his blood was left on her, the scrubbings turned into scratchings until the skin was raw. Then the other me knew it was her blood, giving that deep feeling of accomplishment at washing him down the drain. The soap burned slightly, reassuring her of cleanliness. And when the water turned to its icy cold sting, she shut off the water, knowing that for a little while she would be almost clean on the outside.

With an almost fresh sense on the exterior, she began her lengthy internal cleansing—purging. All of the contents of her stomach must be forced up and out. Continuously purging until nothing was left, just dry heaves. Then came the scrubbings of the mouth—its teeth, its gums, its tongue, all of its tissues. Cleaning until once again the blood seeped from around the teeth, free of particles, lust. And just to ensure her cleanliness, she gargled for long, long periods before risking what she may taste inside her mouth. Any taste other than blood was undesirable. For it was the blood that would tell her how well she had cleaned.

Her mind and body tired, she wished the cleaning was over. But she knew it wasn't. Actually, it would never end until layer after layer of her damaged mind was replenished and restored. His lust was still inside of her, eating away at her, forming clones for birth or for hibernation, always keeping claim on her, regardless of how much she resisted.

She wanted to douche. She needed to douche over and over, reaching each crevice or fold of tissue that might somehow be shaded with his lust. Only the water needed to be hot—very hot—killing the lustful germs being flushed out time after time. Muscles within her legs ached from the abuse and the cleaning. But still she had to continue for what seemed like hours. Finally, she thought herself to be a little less dirty. Scrubbing her genitals over and over, she believed the lustful puddles of sin to have been washed away. Still, she wasn't finished. Oh, how the pain continued with each movement she made. But the me was saying the cleaning must continue. It just could not stop shy of completion.

An enema was needed. One with hot, hot water to purify the bruised and battered tissues damaged from his onslaught. Not just one enema, but many to relax the tense muscles, to soothe the stinging tissues, to wash the blood until sure there was not any of him left, to wash away the passionate crumbs of his evil appetite. Hurriedly, she stepped back into the shower to begin, once again, the scrubbing away of any and all remnants; one more gesture to ensure the least amount of filth having been absorbed by her cells. Once the shower water changed to cold, she could lavish her body with a soft lotion, nurture it and put it to bed for rest.

This almost clean body, internally and externally,

would, through sleep, manage to shelve the trauma neatly in her mind among the crevices, hoping cobwebs and dust would temper their reality. Sleep always helped when the other me's were exhausted, serving to put stability into the devoured soul. That's what the cleaning and recleaning achieved by setting some type of barrier in areas where boundaries were crossed and recrossed. The barrier was in place, time was ticking away, and sadly, the demise of her barrier was also commencing.

Memories—flashbacks! They were the alarm, alerting her of the fallen barrier. Awake, hurting, filthy—internally and externally—she was each of these. The body is slow moving through time when the mind is pounded with furious memories. Racing into the bathroom was too slow as she grabbed bottles of Clorox and alcohol, falling into the shower. Steaming hot water streamed heavily across her body screaming to have its skin yanked from its skeleton. Time was too slow! Her body moved at a snail's pace. Grasping the Clorox, she poured it over her skin, awaiting the deep burning sensation of cleaning her body of the lust left upon it.

Clean! Kill! Pull his lustful sins away! Oh, how hard she cried with her heart, only to find her mind and eyes refusing to join. Somehow it seemed her crying could have made a difference in the filth and frustration she experienced, and yet, her mind simply refused.

His remnants were inside of her, lingering, waiting to oppose the forces of purging. She was tired. It hurt to purge, forcing her to get it right this time. Mixing water and Clorox, she gulped as much as could be tolerated before the purging erupted with projectile force. Watching the substance shoot against the shower wall, there was an acknowledgment of internal cleansing. For the first time in years, she perceived herself as a little more than almost clean. This exhausted and battered body began to see the little light at the end of the tunnel.

Using the Clorox and water, she douched away the awakened lustful components folding over as the stinging pain became too much to endure. Again, there was that sense of being cleaner, and had time allowed, she would have prepared an enema with the same mixture. However, her body, or some force, accommodated the cleaning of the bowel, stinging and burning. It was over—for now.

Slowly, she dabbed the alcohol over her broken skin absorbing it into her broken heart as the trauma was sealed inside her mind, perhaps permanently, perhaps not. More important, the trauma was contained. Neither was it maximizing at this point. The mind was intellectualizing, noting the urgent need to glance quickly at the invisible shelf, clothe the other me in layers of plastic before slipping her gently under the blankets, and for a short time, allow this mind a moment to recoup. The child in all these personalities urged her to clutch her blankie and sleep. The parent continued to wrap the plastic layer after layer. And the adult did nothing, for his power was too great.

CHAPTER 22

I first noticed last week when my mornings were times of vomiting. By noon each day, I was fine. My appetite had increased. With the tenderness of my breasts, I was somewhat concerned. I had been pregnant four months earlier. Could I be pregnant again? My greatest fear! Fear, not because of the pregnancy, but rather, because of the last abortion. Never did I want to endure that experience again. My father had been so brutal, I feared he would repeat his crime. The knife stabbing inside of me was still very vivid in my memory. Surviving that ordeal again was impossible in my thinking.

First, I needed verification if I was pregnant. Should the answer be negative, there would be no problem. Should the answer be positive, arrangements would have to be made for a second abortion. The thought of my being pregnant was sickening. There was no way I would give birth to his child. He would never know if I was pregnant.

With careful planning, I was able to forge my father's signature on an early dismissal pass. I had to learn the fate of my life. Uncomfortable about the entire issue, I drove to a neighboring county for an appointment I had scheduled two days earlier. No one would know me, and chances of my father learning were lessened. Payment would be in cash, and a pseudonym was used. The needed diagnosis would be obtained with no identifiable information. It had taken careful planning, but I had been able to do it.

Driving the distance created anxiety. The drive home would provide me the time to adjust to the news. Locating the office was simple. It looked small, but as long as the necessary diagnosis could be obtained, it did not matter. I was here. Now, all I had to do was walk inside. For a few long minutes, I did nothing. Then I entered in a scared, tense state.

My fear was confirmed. This would not just go away. Now I knew I would have to make arrangements for an abortion. Getting the time away without my father could be a problem. He was always around. Destiny would have to be in my court if I was to pull this off. Something extremely unlikely would have to happen in order for this to work.

Time was passing without any progress. The continual abuse was making life very stressful and very hopeless. The money would be no problem. Getting away without my father would be. Then, one day, as if it had fallen from the sky, my father was scheduling a business trip. The last two weeks in June, he would be away.

Once again, there were plans to be made. Careful plans would be the only key to success. One act without in-depth thought would foil my life once again. The consequences this time would mean the probability of my father repeating his earlier crime. I could not allow this to happen. I concentrated on the plan—nothing else. Careful detailed planning could save me from my father. The primary issue was not the abortion, it was getting through the coming weeks without my father's knowledge. Unknown to him, my father was again the timekeeper, setting the pace he desired without knowledge of the pregnancy.

The plan was finished—carefully finished. My friend and I were to spend the day in New York shopping. No one expected to see us until late that evening. Money was always available to both of us. The shopping had been completed earlier—no one ever checked what we bought. But we had done so just in case. The items were in the trunk of my car. No one ever looked there. The abortion was scheduled. We flew to New York. The airport limousine service drove us to the clinic.

The greatly yearned for abortion was completed. Several hours would have to elapse without any complications before we could leave. We prayed for no complications—that was the strangeness about this. Two Catholics flying out of state for an abortion and then asking God's blessings for no complications. I suppose He listened for there were no problems. However, I did not think about the emotional effects which would surface decades later.

We left New York on schedule and flew home. We checked into a hotel for the rest of the afternoon and early evening. In review of all variables, everything was accounted for—clothes, less cash, elapsed time, no baby. If I made it through the next two days without extreme bleeding, my plan would be successful. Because no one was home to be with me, my friend stayed overnight. For the first time in such a long, long time, something was working out for me. My victory was overshadowed as I thought of abortion as murder, but I could not survive my father if I had chosen otherwise.

My life was much different from that point onward. I knew I had to get out of this house as soon as possible. Any delay would only place me at a disadvantage. My fall enrollment in college was still weeks away. That would be the only exit from this house which would assure me an escape from my rapist. A possibility crossed my mind. A drive to the college would give me my answer.

Again, my friend and I set out to make my life less complicated. If I could start second session summer school, I could move out before my father returned. The only problem I could imagine would be housing for the immediate time. I did not believe my plan would go unfoiled as it had earlier. If these plans worked, I would have to believe my life was getting better.

It worked! I was free! I could not wait to get back in town to start packing. In my excitement, I had forgotten about housing. But my friend did not. I found a small apartment close to campus. After notifying utilities, I sat down to go over my plans again, making sure everything was covered. I had a campus mailbox because of early fall registration. That would be the address given to my parents. The phone number would be unlisted, so I did not have to explain a different address should he ever question. As far as my parents were concerned, I was living on campus. I had covered every possible problem area. They would never know.

Within one week, I was out of the house and away from my rapist. He was very surprised when he returned. However, nothing was said by either of my parents. More and more time was spent away. I varied my schedule so I would not be in any set pattern. This deterred any surprise visits. Academically, I deliberately registered for the most difficult classes, which explained my having to stay on campus so much. No one questioned why I was enrolling early and never was the location of my residence discussed. They assumed I was living on campus in the dorm—they paid for that. Had my rapist known I was living in an off-campus apartment, I think the rapes and the terror would have continued. My survival was only possible if I could get away where he could not assault me anymore. Even now, I question whether he would have continued.

I was too intelligent to say lying works to one's advantage, but this time, it saved me from my rapist. I would partially confess that sin for many years before putting it to rest. Lying was wrong. I knew I would never do it again. The first night, I stared at the ceiling from a bed that I had not been raped in and breathed easily. At the time, I could not imagine the problems that would surface because of the rapes and terror. But for me at this time, I thought all of my problems had disappeared.

CHAPTER 23

Less and less time was spent with my family. I did not miss anything about them or the house. I had made the decision to make a separate life. That meant making decisions about issues and problems with which I had limited or no experience. There were times when I picked up the phone to call and put it back down. Torn between choices and the possibility of reviving the rapes, I spent many days and nights stressed and unsure of my choices. Regardless, I perceived the consequences of my choice to be more pleasant than my father's abuse. I tried to think things through always with a lot of thought.

I felt scared and alone, but not like the scares I remembered in the past. I was beginning to put order and normality into my life. For some reason, perhaps due to my experiences, I failed to realize that the memories do not just go away because he is no longer nearby or raping me. It was to be a few short days before my memories shocked my being with vivid flashbacks, prohibiting peace. But, there was a wonderful peace for those few days—a happy reprieve without worries.

The memories flashed over and over, despite my attempts to push them away, to make them stop, to forget them. They were so real, my father seemed to be in the room, in my dreams, in my head. The escape I thought would come with the move had not. It was too simple to expect them to slip away quietly with no traces to be found. Believing the memories would go away with time, I continued. Never did I think the damage from my father would stay for such a long, long time. I did not realize the full impact of the abuse and its duration. I wanted everything to be normal as it was for others of my peer group. I underestimated the power his memories would have on me in duration, frequency, and intensity.

One of the simple pleasures I enjoyed was having privacy, something I did not have at home. Going to class and returning to peace rather than a rapist was unusual, somewhat uncomfortable. It almost seemed that I should have to endure the abuse to feel like me. To be without it, I found myself in search for something to go wrong and my rapist returning. There was no missing the abuse, but I did need a family, and that was impossible. For now, I would have to be alone, without a place to call home, without a parental safety net, as the need for distance was greater if I wanted to continue without rapes.

Giving up one thing for another was what my life was all about. Sometimes you give up security to keep yourself safe. My mind entertained thoughts of how it must feel to have security and safety intertwined with pleasure. Always it seemed my mind could think of desired qualities in life that were out of my grasp. The brain acknowledged this, but the heart could not—it meant too much had been lost, too much of what I wanted so desperately. I felt impoverished, not of material things, but of simple things.

I cannot remember the last time my father and I sat for a meal, shared conversation, or took a walk under the stars, that he did not rape and terrorize me. I never recall a time that my mother hugged me or even spoke to me nicely. I think the last words she said to me were in the comment she made the night I told her of the abuse. There were no memories of my mother doing anything with me that was pleasant.

Only memories of her looks with penetrating eyes ejecting the hatred in her heart and the abusive dunkings in the toilet.

She was tolerant of me, and I can only surmise that her tolerance stemmed from my father's power. Had it not been for his power, I think she would have killed me due to her intense hate. It is hard to discern if her killing me would have been less traumatic than the abuse. At times, I wonder if I would have rather been killed and not endured the abuse, or am I glad I escaped her into the abuse. Now I am glad to be alive, but during those times, I resented being alive and being raped over and over.

College provided time for my observing and interacting with my peer group. Conversing on most topics was no problem. I had no perception of how dating and men should be addressed appropriately. There was a lot that I needed to learn and would have to learn if I was to go unnoticed. That was my goal—make it through life without anyone knowing of my abuse. Thoughts of what they might think urged me to keep this part of my life totally unknown.

How could I explain this to anyone else if I did not understand it myself? It was too big of a risk to confide this wicked secret, only to have people make comments. I would never be able to understand nor imagine why any father could do these acts, why a mother would allow it, especially when she was knowledgeable of it. How could a child survive such a demonic lifestyle?

For the first time in my life, I was witnessing what the real world and real people were about. I loved the gaiety, the full spirit, the enthusiasm, the friendship of the students, the sharing of clothes, and the darting around, excitedly rushing to dress for a date. I thought how nice it would be to have a date, to have someone who wanted to spend time with me, someone who would share special moments appropriately, a someone to care for me and I for him.

My mind was racing with pleasant thoughts when it suddenly occurred to me that I knew nothing about dating, about males, about rules, about standards. To be so intelligent, I knew absolutely nothing about the art of dating, a vicious game for those who do not know how to play. A game very enticing, but so frightening, I was unsure if I could play or not. Knowing that this was a normal and natural desire was not comforting. I was more uncomfortable with the realization that my peers had several years' experience with this game, and I had none.

How I hated my parents for the stolen years, stolen opportunities, stolen ego. The overwhelming tide of experience had caught up with me, paralyzing my life. I suddenly acknowledged a battle my soul would have to fight eventually if I was to ever be free. It would be a costly battle in many ways.

Therapy crossed my thoughts, to be quickly swept away by the memories of my father. Oh, the qualities in him—terror, power, authority, leverage, money, strength, silence. Within each and every one of these qualities were various degrees, always used in a negative manner. My rich lifestyle had omitted the very basic components on which my soul thrived. The abuse and terror were battles for survival. This would be a battle for happiness, freedom, understanding, life. This road would have many forks along the way with choices and choices and choices, which would be easy and difficult in nature, with ramifications right and left, embellished with desires, tempered with ambivalence.

Life is, indeed, a learning experience with good things and bad things. To be content with life, there needs to be a balance of both. And within that balance, one must strive to acknowledge the bad, but expect the good, to look for the good. There was clear evidence I would learn more than academics these four years. The thought was scary, but inviting, the kind of motivation that instills character and endurance. These years would begin my road of growth—a road essential, planting the seeds leading to the road of therapy and ultimate freedom. A road that was very long, but with perseverance and endurance was obtainable. A road with good and bad evenly tempered with approachable pathways of enhancement or destruction, but definitely a choice.

CHAPTER 24

Life had seemed too long at times, too short at other times, and always confusing. My mind had somehow sealed away a lot of the memories and pain, hoping to someday eternally forget the travesties of years past. With the passage of days, weeks, months, and eventually years, it was carefully, silently tucked away. Six years had passed. I had married and was pregnant. All of the past was exactly that—the past. It was over, never to happen again. With my silence went its burial. Not once did I anticipate its resurrection after all those years.

    I thought my life had become normalized, giving meaning to many events which before now were void episodes of nothing. The disapproval of my family was apparent and well known. He came from the wrong side of town, wasn't career oriented, egocentric, from a lower social class, a shady past, not good enough. To them, he wasn't acceptable. For me and my purpose, he was ideal. The abuse had taken such a devastating toll upon me that it wasn't important how I felt or what I wanted. More important was the need to lash out at them in whatever way available that was both safe and successful. And perhaps a part of me wanted to make it all work just for spite. It's difficult to say if my marriage ever developed love, but it was a safe place temporarily. It was a haven from my father's abuse, for six years anyway.

    The hot water poured heavily across my skin. My hands worked frantically, scrubbing at the filth he left behind. If only I could use a Brillo pad and Clorox, I could get most of it off. It was important that I not let anyone know, so there could not be raw and scratched patches on my body. If he knew, I'm not sure what he would choose to do. I wanted no one to know. I was too ashamed of what he had done. Somehow he had placed me back into his cage to be at his beckon call, to have to submit to his lust and violence. The hurried scrubbing continued until there just wasn't any time left. My husband would be coming home soon to a situation entirely different from what he knew. The secrets of my life were overflowing my brain, causing me to think of the consequences if I spoke out. Fear of the unknown prohibited this truth from being shared. A prohibition that would, through a chain of events, take from me my most cherishable gifts.

Getting dressed, I reflected on the most recent attack. It was June, I had just finished spring quarter a few weeks earlier and was leisurely enjoying the anticipation of the nursery. Life was beginning to mold me into whatever it is that society expects. My father had been appropriate in his behavior during family visits, which had become less and less. It seemed all our lives had become too busy, making visiting more restricted. Perhaps that is what I associated the decreased family time to, convincing myself that life's unfairness just may have come into balance at last.

It was early afternoon when he rang the bell. I had just put my nephew down for his nap, hoping that my father would not stay because of that. It appeared he knew when to stop by in order to consummate his plan. He wasn't subtle with his demands, but rather blunt as he stated what and how he was about to exert his power over me. Horror filled my mind as disbelief pounded strongly from cell to cell, acknowledging negotiations were not a possible solution to this problem.

If I chose to not submit, my husband would be told of all the years he and I had "participated" in sexual games. Fear swelled my mind with his demeaning statements of time after time in which I initiated sex not only with him, but with his guests also. I knew he would boast about his exploitations, probably telling everyone that I asked for his sexual attentions, that I approached him, that I was indeed all those horrible names he called me. But most of all, my greatest fear that I would be forced back home with him to return to my former life of abuse.

My mind simply stopped. I felt like a prisoner with my father as warden. Running away wasn't possible. This could not be laughed off. He was intent on taking whatever he desired. Suddenly, all those little girl fears were back, with different meanings and implications. Immediately, suicide possessed my thoughts, despite the tiny creature inside of me. The alcohol breath of my father nauseated me, or perhaps it was his demands. Regardless, I felt weak, destroyed. I begged for him to please go away, not to rape me anymore. His wicked laugh, many years old, filled the air. I was destined to be raped once again. Were his threats more powerful? There wasn't time to think.

Numbness was seizing her body leaving her mind in search for that invisible shelf filed back in the corners of darkness, longing to cling to it once again, grasping that familiar comfort it had always provided. I thought of it much like the feeling a child receives when its loving parents cradle it in their arms. That was a feeling I did not know, but had surmised it to be probably the best feeling in the world.

It was time for splitting off again. Six years had passed since he last violated her, forcing her to question if she would survive. The passage of the years had convinced her all the rapings were behind her, forgotten, somehow buried beyond recovery. It had been a silent burial, acknowledging no one, nothing, as its seal of silence engulfed another silent secret.

She felt like a rodent in search of crumbs in a barren room. The hatred, frustration of the situation raged through her tissues until finally settling in the pit of her stomach, having been swallowed, securing its silence. Erecting that needed barrier to survive was difficult. The situational factors had changed—she was an adult now, but deep inside she wasn't. Sensing his closeness, she focused in on the other me's—their numbers, sizes, purposes. She knew she was splitting off again. It had been a long, long time since the last splitting. Lining each of them up in a single file, she meticulously aligned each, starting over each time one of the me's moved, spoke, smiled, cried. Over and over she earnestly examined the beast who had created the terror, the pain, the splitting off of all of the me's.

He ripped her clothing away, laughingly making his nasty comments. She worried about the baby. Would he hurt it, kill it, abort it? Lost in her thoughts, she failed to notice his halted attack. His wicked laugh sent her mind back years as he removed a condom, putting it in place.

Grabbing a handful of hair, he said, "I don't want any of your damn diseases, whore!"

Oddly, there was a small amount of relief, for now his ejaculation would not be felt against her tissues, freeing her of some of his filth. Without further hesitation, he entered her, squeezing her breasts, moaning, raising his hand so to strike her face. Angrily, he demanded her participation, breathing heavily in her face as he pushed her legs into her chest. The alcohol and his thrusting pains were precisely those of so long ago. Surely, it would not be long now until she could be alone.

It would soon be over if she just didn't fight, resist, struggle. Passivity was needed. Without haste, the other me assumed that passive role, yielding an avenue for her rapist's gratification, yet prohibiting her participation. The other me just lay there wearing nothing but the blank look upon her face. She glanced down at the other me, grateful that it was her chosen to be the recipient of the rape, saving her once again.

The other me knew her role as did all the others before her. It was no different. The other me's simply survived blow to blow, rape to rape, terror to terror, waiting for the end. Perhaps it was shock that settled and stilled this other me to a deeper pitch, defeated by disbelief. Her mind groped through memories long, long ago, one by one lingering upon the worst, discerning the variable, affording survival, then resting intensely on the me's, one or two that were birthed for happiness. They were the way she wanted and needed for her world to be. It was only now that the importance of the happy me's was evident. At that time, she perceived the happy other me's as what life was for other little girls, but they were, in actuality, the nurturance that was otherwise unavailable. The passage of years absent of the abuse from him troubled the other me's with baffling thoughts, confusion, pain.

Suddenly, she focused in on the small life inside her. Would he abort it? Damage it? She screamed within her mind, erecting a thicker and thicker barrier. His skin touched hers, his saliva on her nude body, his breath tainted with alcohol. How she wanted him away from her, out of her life! Wanting to push him away pounded through her head. She had put a life together, and now he was back, ready to destroy it all.

Her mind started listing brand-name products for cleaning. Over and over she named them within her mental ear. Then when this was all polished with perfection, certain that none had been omitted, all were alphabetized. The progression of time allowed for repetition; and the compelling force perfected each repetition, always going back to the beginning when an error was made.

Cleaning was important; and for now, the listing and categorizing was vital for the other me. She would need to do much cleaning as quickly as possible. Within her mind she searched the laundry shelves for the cleansers—the heavy-duty kind—to burn away the scum left on and within her cells. Clorox! Her mind had found it there upon the second shelf. It was a large size, so she would be able to clean and reclean. When the skin was red, swollen, and stinging, she would be almost clean—a pleasing, pleasing thought.

As his filth poured out and his nasty talk reached its peak, the other me realized she could not clean to the depth she desired. Doing so would reveal what had happened. The other me knew she would not be present if confronted with the raw skin. It would be another of the many me's that would surface to the demanding questions. Questions that this other me would not be able to respond to and still survive. This was one good reason for so many me's—always one or more to step in when a crisis arose.

There had become so many splittings of the core. Would the splittings ever stop? And when it did stop, would there be so many of them that the core would no longer be? A subtle acceptance came about this other me as she relinquished the yearnings to scrub the filth away. There would be no need for the strong cleansers, for her rapist had again placed her in a situation in which what she wanted to do could not be done.

All hope destroyed, this other me transferred to still another me—that little toddler standing between the wall and the toilet crunched into that corner, filling it with all her fear. How horrible it must have been for her, so small, so young, so hopeless. Yet, she made it through without the cognitive experiences of the other me's. How frightened that one must have been, knowing that her tyrant ultimately controlled her basic necessities—food, water, clothing, shelter, safety.

Why didn't the tyrant just drown her in the toilet? Would the other me ever understand why? How did the other me have the endurance to live? And then, clearly and quietly the answer crept into the older me's mind. Her silence! Had she cried, talked, whimpered, her life would have been ended. Perhaps that was the commonality among the many me's—silence. It served as the saving variable time and time again. That is what needed to happen now. Leaving the toddler alone, she transferred herself back to the moment.

The frustration was escalating, forcing more self-control, which meant this other me would be replaced by the victim. That could not be. With a deep breath and a nauseated stomach, she sealed her eyes within her mind as baby kittens at birth. The ears simply lapped forward preventing the sounds of the room. The mouth was tightly and neatly stitched shut with big black cords just in case some of the words elected to be voiced. The blackness of the cords would deter them should the mind forget and attempt to speak.

Remaining silent was not what she wanted to do. She wanted to fight back, to scream, to claw, to bite. This other me suddenly found parts of the victim interfering with her survival strategy. Never had this happened before and neither could it be allowed to continue. It had been the detachment that assured silence, which in turn assured survival. She could not be consumed by this conflict at this moment, for there was too much fear the other me would not stay to absorb the pain, but rather, pass it onto her, the real little girl of decades past.

As he laughingly dressed, he gave instructions to remain quiet, to shower, to act normal when my husband came home that day. Walking into the bathroom to arrange his appearance, he threatened to destroy my marriage if I found it difficult to remain silent. This threat was my first realization that my planned marriage to reap vengeance upon my parents had actually reaped vengeance upon me. I hurt them by marrying the one person they found inadequate. However, the ultimate hurt was his rape of me. Other than a slight chuckle now and then, my rapist remained virtually silent.

After ten to twelve minutes in the bathroom, he walked into the hallway looking at the filth left behind. His eyes were plastered upon me as he whispered, "Don't worry, baby, Daddy will be back for more."

Thoughts were racing, trembling cell after cell of the brain, as they always did just prior to splitting off, only there was no image forming. No image, no feeling, no hope, just numbness in a desecrated void. He was finished now, and soon perhaps, he would leave. After threats of what he could and would do, he left the other me lying in the remnants of his lust, making her and her life obsolete.

Oh, how intently she wished to split off once again, but there were already so many of them, she wasn't sure she could accommodate another. Instead, all the me's treaded upon her mind, occupying her thoughts as she moved from one task to another in preparation for disguising the violation. Whether the disguise would be temporary or permanent, no one knew. The one sure fact was that none of the other me's were ready to discuss this evil. Some of them even thought the silence would lessen the brutal impact. After a plan of strategy had been devised, she and the other me's would decide when the silence could be lifted. Until that time, she would pretend nothing had ever happened today. When and if the time came to tell, one of them might.

The shower had been nice—cleansing. His last words echoed in my ears indirectly letting me know over and over the power he had in my life. Shocked, mortified, alone; and my husband was en route home. There were many things I needed to do—clean, sleep, check on the baby, remain silent, and clean, clean, clean. If only I could scrub his rape away before... I had to think what to do and in which order.

A soft whimpering cry caught my attention, suddenly giving me importance. Thinking of the tiny life inside of me, I gently lifted this little child temporarily in my care, feeling the warmth of its body, which somehow tempered the attack with nurturance; and yet, this little life was totally dependent upon me for safety. I held it close for a long, long time, savoring the baby smell that lingered on my clothes.

It would be okay. It had to be okay, otherwise I would become his sexual ploy once again. My thoughts were burdened. In minutes my husband would be home. I had not decided what to do at this point. My drifting mind knew I needed to have some explanation if questioned.

The previous months had not been easy for us. Several times we came close to separating. I had suspected him of having had an affair just prior to this. There had been so much interference from his family, always making plans for us without consultation, always expecting our presence upon demand. And then, there was the hatred, despise from my family. If ever a marriage needed space, this one did, and no one was willing to allow that. The baby's presence reduced my stress, as if my safety net, but that was about to come to a close. And once the baby was gone, I was unsure of how I might handle the day's events.

My anticipation ended quickly. As I was about to prepare dinner, my husband stormingly entered the den, demanding to know who had been there that day.

Shocked, I shouted back, "Just us!"

Angrily, he shoved me down onto the floor, grabbing

my clothing at the chest, harshly screaming, "What's a rubber doing in the toilet?"

The slug to my head delayed my response, allowing him time to continue. "Who have you been fucking?"

Holding my head, I replied, "No one!"

He continued to accuse me of seeing someone else, threatening to tell the families of what he had found. Something within me encouraged him to do so, to question both my sister and my father, that I had nothing to do with that, and if I ever did want to have an affair, I would certainly cover my tracks.

And when the pain became too much, she split off once again. Each of the me's comforted her, one by one moving in and out of her mind as needed. None actually announcing their arrival nor departure, just a tug at her mind in one of the many crevices that served as incubators when the other me's were sleeping. Bouncing from age to age, time to time, me to me, she awaited her destiny. Guessing that destiny was futile, for she already knew her future, it was her past; the chances of its changing were nonexistent. It almost seemed that way back in the rear on the dustiest shelf of a crevice covered with cobwebs, someone had recorded that destiny. In order for it to change, life would also have to be altered. That just wasn't going to happen, not for her anyway.

Hours had passed since my husband left. He still was gone. Frustrated, defeated, I went to bed. It had been a long day with much unpleasantness and not a hell of a lot to look forward to, considering the situational factors. The door slammed, announcing his return. His thundering footsteps alerted my senses to an onslaught that I did not know if I could survive and from which I had no place to go for safety.

Suddenly, he threw me from the bed, telling me I was a whore, a slut, demanding to know my lover's name. The alcohol on his breath reminded me of my attacker. His senseless questioning continued; the answers he wanted, I did not have, and the answers I had, he did not want. Brutally, he beat my body with his fists for what seemed like hours. As the numbness filled my cellular structure, it also filled the mind that knew I would be the loser, regardless which route was chosen.

When all the beating subsided, this same man nurtured the wounds he had inflicted, promising not to hurt me ever again, sincerely apologizing. The tears streaming down his face made his apology more authentic. It's difficult to discern if it was believable or if I just accepted it rather than risk the consequences should he find the truth. He had stopped for now, and that was the important issue. Sleep had overtaken him, leaving me to weather the early morning hours, wondering what his next move might be and how to survive him with the least amount of scarring. Perhaps within the early morning rays of light, I could find my answer.

Flying through the air, I awakened. Again, his fists hit heavily upon me. His anger, precisely that of my father's, directed in its entirety at me. There was no resistance on my part, no fight to be found anywhere within me. Instead, that old void feeling within a shell was all there was. It was the same shell, same feeling I had as a child. Suddenly and without warning, my world had changed once again as it had so many times in this long walk of destruction. My mind was echoing his questions of the night, but absorbing all my concentration, deterring him, as he reiterated questions at this time. He demanded I confront both my sister and my father regarding the condom, to which I refused. Some little voice inside told me he still would not believe anything I reported back to him. When he threatened to address them directly, I agreed that would be a good course of action.

It was several days later when the issue arose once again. Instantly, my eyes fell to the bruises decorating my body.

Would it all start happening again? Whether he had actually confronted either of them or not was unknown. I no longer believed the words he spoke, but if he was being honest, my father had once again betrayed me, for he was reported to have denied being there on that day.

Parts of me wondered at times if this denial was valid, and if it was, did he deny that as a vindictive gesture of punishment for my marrying him. Whatever his motive, it was clear I had become the recipient of my very own vengeance, as my marriage did not prevent this rape and my husband had used another's lust for abusing me. There are some things that just have no meaning, no logic, no hope. And there are those who just do not seem to know when to stop the torture of others.

Why was she born? Why? It did not make sense that anyone would be born to live this life. She had always been the recipient of the hate of her family. How she diligently searched for its origin, not understanding how anyone could have done any deed obligating this type of punishment.

The pain and swelling in her face reminded her of the present. One of the other me's appeared to take over her as she vaguely recalled the battering fists. Were those the fists of her rapist or her husband? Her face was becoming tighter and tighter, with the shooting pain increasing from bottom to top. Oh, well, it wasn't important, but they probably were from her husband. Faintly, she recalled his verbal and physical attacks, which seemed at times to be a constant companion.

Where was death? How did it always escape her? Would she ever get to have that wonderful experience? Oh, the release that death would bring! It was an obsession, but one she was just unable to be successful with in the past.

Now she must focus on what would make her feel better, even if it meant suicide. If she could make it work, it would bring completion to the issue. No more rapes, no more fists, no more questions, no more thoughts. It seemed the best of the available options. Please, let her find the courage to do it right this time. And with the help of the other me's, she would find that needed element for suicide. She was being cheered onward by the voices inside, reassuring her of the peace, the withdrawal from life's bitter edge, which could never get to her once she died. The thoughts, if they could be applied, were soothing. It would indeed be much, much better not to have to suffer at their expense anymore.

Only when the young life inside of her crossed her mind did her spirits fall. Murdering an innocent life was less acceptable to her heart and mind than the abuse and its ramifications. If the baby died, then she could do it. That way, she would not be transgressing upon a defenseless child as they had against her. It was that day and that desired decision that created another splitting off—a new other me. It was to be the me obsessed with suicide, always thinking of a plan to be worked out so the most minute details would be resolved. This other me always in reserve for the day, the hour when acceptance of a life without hope could no longer be tolerated. The hours when a tormented soul could be quietly and finally put to an eternal rest.

CHAPTER 25

Strategies composed so much of life, giving it complexities that could not be avoided. Dealing with these complexities provided division among the players. Perhaps man's ultimate goal was to prepare for crises before they arose, and somewhere along this course of destruction, someone had reiterated that premise. Or perhaps she just needed to justify that which she yearned for so many times, but was unable to obtain. Regardless, she had created another me that dealt only with suicide. This one was to a much greater degree oriented toward suicide, while the previous ones had other issues of relevance. This other me was more meticulous, more consistent, more obsessed with devising a successful suicide plan.

Always, she yearned for an escape from the pain of living. She perceived her ultimate need to be that of freedom from the memories, which awaken her to this day, forcing the mind into a reliving of the horror that created her flight. Sadly, she recalled the many times she attempted to discard the pain of his lust and failed. It had been a roller coaster of hell, ups and downs, compelling a distorted mind and despised body from decade to decade, always alone.

But the aloneness was desired. It was the interference by the other players that brought devastation upon her. The suicidal other me did not wish to interact with anyone or anything. She wanted to be without them and their violations.

Carefully, she arranged a strategy that would include each of the other me's with a designated role, making sure that, daily, everyone was preparing for the eventual end. With preparation, it would be easier to close the final chapter of each me, thus allowing the completion of the deaths. Only when all were put to rest could she commence her plan.

It wasn't that she thought of suicide every minute. There had been times when she did not—sometimes as long as several days or weeks—but always when her mind relinquished, it did so to the suicidal mode. And when this occurred, it was not the abuse that she focused on, but rather, all the things she had missed out on because of the abuse. She wanted those years recaptured, relived. There was a need internally to be hugged and cradled, to be rocked and read to by parents, not caretakers, to be loved and cherished for just being theirs.

These were the ideas, the feelings she perceived as forever lost, destroyed, not only by the abuse, but also by the abandonment. But perhaps most of all, she yearned for the safety a child should have, needs to have, a safety net without holes, a safety net without any strings, conditions attached. This internal yearning birthed her desire for suicide. These were the times she craved her suicide, believing that only through this act could she finally have control of her life.

There were times when she did not dwell on this issue, for any number of reasons, but even then, the thought would linger briefly within her mind as she recounted the course of the day just before bedtime. The recounting created a diversion of the memories that would plague her nightmare-filled sleep to taunt her endlessly. She could not discern whether there was greater sorrow in the recounting of the day, focusing on the missing joys, or on the terror of the memories that still to this day provoke all senses, engulfing and lashing them with nightmare after nightmare. And did it really matter? The ramifications of both were beyond acceptance, beyond belief, beyond discussion.

And then there were the times when sleep deprivation overtook the suicidal me, leading her farther and farther into this forest of death. This was when the voices increased dramatically, chanting death statements, controlling all she did day to day and well into the night, as if it were a time of judgment, citing all the failures she endured, the lack of love shown to her, the total peace she would find as she entered the forest of death, progressing to its core, where she along with all the other me's would meet death, becoming as one never to exist again.

The walk into the forest of death was comforting, hearing the voices urge her to heighten her pace, to bury the memories, to finally be a winner! Compelling music accompanied, increasing its beat with the rhythm and demands of the voices. Their chanting was monumental, awaiting her depthful plunge into death. They crowded in on all sides, moving her along the path. Every face wore a smile, the kind that is luring, despite its reasoning, comfortable, despite its origin, needed like a parent's acceptance, like a parent's love. The solitude they offered was nonresistant, too good in thought to resist, too inconceivable to discount.

Step by step, she continued her walk, acknowledging within her mind just how different it would be when her cells had ceased to function, how quiet the air would become, how she would no longer yearn for the missed moments, no longer dwell upon those yearnings. She would, indeed, be nothing. During brief moments, perhaps seconds, she thought how sad it was that she had been nothing, such a waste.

Subtly, one of the other me's sidled up alongside of her, silently allowing her warmth to mesh with the suicidal me. The warmth was nurturing, not demanding, in its efforts to allure her mind, halting the steps to death, guiding her back toward the entrance to the forest of death and eventually out to safety. This other me knew how to appeal to her many me's, softening the harsh, defeating ones, to provide a cradle of hope as a focus when life just gets to be too much.

This me was the seven-year old, adorned in fresh white clothing, curls, and a gentle face always with a warm and inviting smile. This is what she had always wanted to be, but had only been able to find it through the other me. When this other me was present, she made most of them feel they were in a comfort zone. A zone where danger and death were obsolete, where there was hope, and where there would be a place for her and someone to care. Often, retrospectively, she questioned if this was truly a welcomed time, or was it just a delay in the unavoidable finality, allowing more and more unhappiness to manifest itself. Whatever the reasoning, if any reasoning was in order, this was the other me that was always in her darkest nightmares. Sadly, this one ray of light was many times replaced by the other aggressive me's. It was as if a chance of escape had been dangled before her and then, suddenly, withdrawn. With the last flickers of this little ray of light, sadness overwhelmed her heart.

As quickly as her walk into the forest of death had halted and she was on her way out, the suicidal thoughts returned, telling her again of the joys that had eluded her, never to be captured at any expense. It was the four-year-old, dressed in morbid black, that spoke, always cunning with the justifications of suicide, so confident, so manipulative. The forest welcomed her back. This was a familiar walk, traveled so often in the past; it felt like an old friend, someone that would help. The forest would be there eternally awaiting the final plunge from life into death.

There was disagreement with the other me's on whether life was tolerable or not. Many of them thought not, while a few thought the struggle would end before long, making it all worthwhile. Perhaps that was one of the reasons for keeping the me's separate—too much conflict to function as one. And at many times, too many to be housed within one soul, one mind. The monumental conflict created by them all mandated too much time to be spent on issues that created pain. It was difficult to think she would abandon those few me's who believed in her, but at the same time, the solitude offered by those me's who urged her to destroy the vessel so greatly abused by the very ones who should have loved her was tempting. The latter was more promising and, for the most part, more acceptable.

Long hours occupied with these thoughts had grown into days, weeks, months, years, and then, a lifetime. An unacceptable life should yield an acceptable death. But it did not. Each time she was ready to complete this task, another me popped in to conflict an even more unresolvable situation. Although truly yearning to die, she often experienced a tugging at her inner self, which was a compelling drive to survive. There were days she thought of these moments as hope, only to learn later these were the voices of the me's.

This pronounced conflict fueled the suicidal other me beyond limits, becoming an eternal source resultantly creating a self-destructive beast. Winning was supposedly somewhere in life, perhaps hidden among the varied refuges from the world's population. Should it be found, it may be a gatherable item for later use, but more probably the battles of daily living would obscure her search. Always, she failed at her attempts to die, leaving other me's filled with remorse, while some smiled briefly at another perceived victory.

This me was different from those formed earlier. This one was a composite of them all—all the emotions, all the abuse, all the pains, the hatred, the frustration, the disgust, the tears. Yes, the tears having been locked away many years earlier had settled somewhere within her, hoping someday to find that small outlet providing relief.

At times it appeared these other me's were actually different emotions that were housed together in the suicidal me. The validity of that was irrelevant, for experiencing the emotions in a detached state always brought her back to the one with so many other me's. Because of this, the suicidal me was convinced life had nothing to offer except death. The courage it was taking for her to live was just too harsh to endure as each day brought to mind the many moments she had missed, but yearned to enjoy. Death, and only death, could prevent with complete certainty the recurrence of these yearnings.

CHAPTER 26

His death came unexpectedly. The news arrived; I felt no emotions. I had experienced so many emotions with him or because of him, but at this moment I did not feel anything. The immediate days thereafter were just as emotionless. There was no change in me. Making funeral arrangements were ordinary as if a part of my every day. There were no tears, no hate, no anger, no relief—nothing. I never viewed the body, nor did I have that desire. Participating in this scene was bothersome. My mind reflected through the years earlier to that time when I vowed never to feel tears upon my cheeks.

My emotions were becoming ambivalent. A part of me wanted to cry, not for the loss of him, but for the loss of me, to smile and say good-bye for the final time to the beast of my life. Part of me wanted to call upon all those tears that I had hidden away so carefully deep within my affective self. Part of me wanted to cognitively delete his memories. But so doing would delete the major portion of my own life. Part of me wanted to speak out on behalf of, and in protection of, all little girls in the world. Part of me wanted to hate, to destroy. Part of me wanted to scream. I wanted to sleep, but most of all, I wanted to be unborn, safe from the erupted terrors.

Giggles and smiles had gone away so many years ago, I no longer looked for their return. Laughing was no longer a part of me. My belief in the goodness of people had died. I did not trust. My hunt was for the negative in life. Always I had looked for ways to die. I was unsure if this meant I could stop trying to die.

The funeral was an inconvenience, an imposition upon my time. There was no desire to be present. There were no feelings left and had not been for such a long time. I wondered if that was wrong. I wondered if he ever regretted raping me, or did he judge his actions to be acceptable.

Thinking of the abuse created frustration in me, the kind of frustration that needed to be processed, expressed. But I couldn't do that. He was dead, and my telling of the abuse would be useless. It was a secret that he and I had shared for many years. No one would believe me. My mother had not—a fact my father's wicked laugh boasted of always. Some things are better left alone, much like a sleeping dog. That was a good metaphor. I was much like his dogs, captivating of his attention, obedient to his commands, vessels for his pleasures, possessions of his. The difference being in the treatment. His dogs were treated more appropriately. Incest was unacceptable. It created years of pain and terror intermixed with self-hate and guilt.

The words of the priest halted my thinking. I hated being here. It was a waste of time. It was such a feelingless gesture that the event held no significance for me. Yes, it ended the abuse from him, but it did not end the abuse of his memories. He was no longer a mortal threat, but was now a haunting spirit that would control and manipulate me for years after his death. The bad times had canceled out all the good, probably by a large ratio.

I kept telling myself that children are more adaptable to life's demands than they are perceived. I suppose for some things that is true, but it wasn't applicable to this. The scars would forever remain of when I was forced to play adult as a child. I wonder if I was ever loved. I say yes at times and no at other times. Another unanswered question. My mind was tired. My life was tired. My heart was numb.

Mentally, I listed items for the supermarket. A very detailed list of essentials for cleaning, not for regular cleaning, but heavy cleaning when you want to destroy all the bacteria, eliminating all traces of the silent evil. I needed the list for me and for the memories. Scrubbings in the shower came back to my mind. The soap—the Clorox, burning deep within my raw skin! The washing away of all traces of him. He had wasted so much of my life, forcing me to do acts so repulsive, I wanted the filth off of me.

There was no way. I wanted to pull the skin off, making all those horrible rapes vanish forever. I had thought that with his death would come that erasing of my memories. Instead, my being was inundated by them. These very memories became parasitic upon my soul just as they had done when I was younger. Processing and surviving the memories wasn't any easier now. At times, it appeared there was less control over these hauntings as I aged.

His death wasn't anything like I thought it would be. I had frequently told myself this event would bring the full release from our destructive secret. No one would ever know, because he was dead. And I would never tell. He had terrorized me into silence. He had hurt me time after time. I promised myself to never experience this torture again. I would make my life different with his abuse absent. These were the promises I had made as an adolescent. It became my survival incentive. It was to be revealed as one of the more foolish assumptions I had assimilated. The dark, dark secret embedded in me had eaten away at my internal self. Optimism was not a part of my life; pessimism had devoured my soul.

The weeks following his death were much worse than earlier. I missed my father greatly. I wanted to love him for those wonderful times absent of abuse, and hate him for violations that had taken such a heavy toll on a child, creating no will to live. His rapes had changed me from a happy child to a child with no hope, no desire, no motivation, no will, and, most of all, no spirit. It left a child trying to find logic in his actions and why a mother offered no protection.

With the passage of the years, I made a very conscious decision that no one anywhere in this world could be trusted; that the purpose of my life must be representative of evil, for if God loved me, He would not permit this to happen; that men, all men, were abusive; that women allowed their children to be used as sexual ploys; that terror was the larger portion of everyone's life; that there was nothing in life to be cherished because it was all shared, and most of it without your permission. Nothing was right in this world, nothing could be reversed.

Yes, I lived every day of my life looking for death—going through the daily functions, but always, always looking for death. My frustration ate away at me. Anger was wrong—my father, my rapist, my terrorist had said it was. So I swallowed my anger and let it sit quietly in the pit of my stomach, creating ulcers and pain, but never being expressed. It was much like my obsessive-compulsive behaviors. It was there, but not acknowledged according to its validity. Rather recognized as frustrations to be tightly controlled and hidden from everyone.

It was difficult to accept life as anything different than that which I had experienced. It was not that I believed everyone had been abused, but that I could not comprehend what having never been abused would have been like. I did not know how it felt to have had a good affectual life with responsible parents. My mind felt confused. The memory of my childhood was unclear today—maybe it could be recalled tomorrow.

The priest was standing in front of me, speaking. Walking to the coffin, I recited a prayer, made the sign of the cross and departed. My departure was to be a permanent one. My mind flashed back to that horrible night when I watched the lid to another coffin coldly shut. I felt uncomfortable with my rapist now caged, much as the hatred in my heart.

Never have I gone back for even a look. I do not know what it looked like when it was finished. I feared having to look at this grave. The chance that I would remember more vividly the terror he had inflicted upon me prevents my return. I often think of the grave and wonder if anyone ever visits it, or if it is like so many things today that go unnoticed. How sad it must be to have no one to visit your grave, no one to place flowers on it, and no one who wants to remember.

His death has placed him in the same setting I have found myself—alone! The one person I loved with all my heart, I no longer wanted to think about. My hero, who hurt me over and over, never to hurt the way I have, was dead. He will not know the pain of someone when their hero tosses them to the enemy. There will be no way to reverse the damage; to share happy times or have a hug from someone who loves you. The sadness is overwhelming.

Sometimes I can forget about the grave, but never, never can I forget the memories that have destroyed me, encasing my mind in damaged shield after damaged shield. Some things last forever and that is good, but the eternity placed upon his memories is not good.

Some days are better than others, and some days I do not want to get out of bed. There are still times when I want to die and times when I plan my death. And there have been times when I have started to implement my death and stopped for some reason unknown to me. There is sadness in my heart everyday, not because of the abuse, but because I miss the hugs and smiles that were not a part of my life;

early morning strolls; sitting in the sunshine; looking for four-leaf clovers; feeding ducks; laughter and silliness; making shapes out of clouds; sharing the same chocolate chip cookie; friendship, love, kindness; walks on a rainy day; sharing and not sharing moments of reading one's heart in silence; rainbows amidst sunny skies; and always believing you have found the pot of gold at the beginning of the rainbow. My being yearns to cry out because my parents were not the pot of gold at the beginning of my rainbow....

... someday, perhaps, I will cry and cry, realizing that my pot of gold was not with my parents, but rather with myself.

AFTERWORD

The writing of this trauma has taught the me in control that there is hope. The yearnings are just what they are called—yearnings. They are not actions or plans or strategies. They are the desires of the heart and mind in conflict, regardless of their origin. A yearning for death does not make that act possible; and I have found, time after time, I cannot take my life even when the pain of all the past creases my growth and tarnishes my mind. Oh, how grateful I am now my soul has struggled to survive. For in that survival, I can be assured of happy times to be cherished forever.

There is no way of recovering the past, no way of changing the past. Lost time cannot be recaptured. However, I am young enough to find many cherishable moments; to find the true meaning to life; to find the good in the adversity; and to integrate all the me's into one solid core.

Life is worth living, despite the adversities that complicate everyone's life. What was once overwhelming to the suicidal me is now viewed from a broader perspective. There is a challenge arising that I desire to address and achieve. Never did I realize the time, the energy, the pain to be encountered during this integration. Despite all the trauma, all the humiliation, all the pain, and all the terrors, there is goodness in this world if one is willing to search and endure. Perhaps this is why life has become more than just acceptable; that giving up on life had been their intended message; that I had faced more terror than they; that my beating this, through therapy, hospitalization, pharmacology, or whatever else was recommended, was the goal I had to focus upon daily. By succeeding at integrating the many me's into one, I will be winning a victory they could never take from me.

My mind has cried many times for the little girl in me. My eyes have not; but my heart is confident that as the integration is completed, I will be able to carefully, and painfully, relive each and every violation upon the different me's. And in so doing, I will be ready and able to eternally merge each me, permanently placing them as part of the one me to finally and happily walk forth.